A trio of Vulcan B.1s in the guise that the type first entered frontline service during 1957. From then, Avro's mighty delta served until the K.2 tankers of 50 Squadron were paid off in March 1984. After that, the Vulcan enjoyed eight years displaying to appreciative audiences all over Britain until September 1992, when the RAF called it a day. The Vulcan to the Sky Trust determined that the type still had life in it, this time as a civilian: this special publication tells the story of that incredible achievement. KEY COLLECTION

GW00702993

Contents

Edited by: Ken Ellis,
    with thanks to Nigel Price and Steve Beebee
Contributing Author: Hugh Trevor
With thanks to: The Vulcan to the Sky Team, especially
Richard Clarke, Ian Homer, Michael Trotter and Dr Robert
Pleming

Art Editor: Mike Carr
Chief Designer: Steve Donovan

Production Editor: Sue Blunt
Deputy Production Editor: Carol Randall
Production Manager: Janet Watkins

Advertisement Manager: Alison Sanders
Advertising Production: Debi McGowan
Group Advertisement Manager: Brodie Baxter

Marketing Executive: Shaun Binnington
Marketing Manager: Martin Steele
Commercial Director: Ann Saundry

Managing Director and Publisher: Adrian Cox
Executive Chairman: Richard Cox

Contacts
Key Publishing Ltd, PO Box 100, Stamford, Lincs, PE9 1XQ.
Tel 01780 755131
Email flypast@keypublishing.com
www.keypublishing.com

Distribution: Seymour Distribution Ltd, 2 Poultry
Avenue, London EC1A 9PP. Tel 020 74294000
Printed by: Warners (Midland) plc, The Maltings,
Bourne, Lincs, PE10 9PH

Published by: Key Publishing Ltd – see above
Printed in England

55 Years, 8 Seasons

Dr Robert Pleming has been part of the Vulcan project since its inception. Ken Ellis talked to him about the world's most powerful warbird

A public relations executive could not ask for more: the Vulcan was 55 years old and had entered its eighth display season – *and* its serial number ended in 558! It was copy made in heaven; the press release could wend its electronic way to the media.

By the time these words are read, Vulcan XH558 will have flown for the last time. There are many people that could be quizzed about this gargantuan project, but there is one standout candidate and he can add to the numbers game.

Dr Robert Pleming has been involved for a staggering 18 years and, as XH558 enters its next phase, it looks as though he will still have a major part to play in the delta's future.

From the beginning of his association with XH558, Robert has been perpetually busy; but that is the default setting for everything he does. In the days running up to the delta's much anticipated farewell 'tour' in early October 2015 his list of commitments was massive. He was very pleased to let me interview him, but it would have to be during a 40-minute slot while he cruised up the A34. Thanks to Robert's hands-free car phone, the inquisition could be fitted in.

Robert has always had an interest in aviation, mostly from the technological aspect. His doctorate is in nuclear physics, so the Vulcan's role of Armageddon-bringer has specific significance to him. Aged 17 he was granted an RAF scholarship, learning to fly on Cessna 152s at Luton, and he loved every minute. He "keeps his hand in" and is pleased to find that the skills are "there forever, they always come back to you".

> "ONCE I'D STARTED, I FOUND IT WAS IMPOSSIBLE TO STOP; AT EVERY STAGE THERE WAS A COMPULSION TO STAY ON TO THE NEXT PHASE, AND SO ON."

The air force was not the career path he adopted: it lay with high-tech, heavy-pressure posts at IBM and then Cisco. But by the mid-1990s Robert had determined that he didn't want to work in that sphere any longer and new challenges beckoned.

EVEREST OF RESTORATIONS

He had been one of the tens of thousands who had signed the petition to pressurise the Ministry of Defence to keep the Vulcan Display Flight running, but of course this was to no avail. David Walton acquired XH558 and it settled in at its new home at Bruntingthorpe, Leicestershire, in March 1993.

Always one to get involved in things others shy away from, Robert was intrigued by the idea of reversing the MoD's decision and putting the Vulcan back in the air – as a civilian. "This would be the Everest of aircraft restorations," he declared, adding that

he figured he would devote two years to the scheme and then find another niche in the world of commerce. "Once I'd started, I found it was impossible to stop. At every stage there was a compulsion to stay on to the next phase, and so on."

Three elements concentrated Robert's mind to take on this demanding task. He realised the Vulcan's importance in world aviation heritage and that it should not be allowed to fade away. The engineering and technological achievement appealed to the physicist in him; in just 11 years, Avro's gifted design team had progressed from the Lancaster to the Vulcan. This was an incredible leap, the like of which has never been repeated. Finally, he was aware of the huge public feeling for the delta.

These all combined to convince him that XH558 *had* to get back into the sky.

MAKING SURE OF A 'YES'

From an engineering point of view, restoring the Vulcan represented known territory and there was no point dwelling on it. A regulatory mountain needed to be conquered first. In 1997 Robert pored through the Civil Aviation Authority (CAA) regulations and realised that, without the manufacturer on his side, the scheme was a dead duck. The name Avro had long since

been subsumed and at that time it was British Aerospace (BAe – BAE Systems from 1999) that needed to be persuaded.

Gathering a team of specialists around him, they all devoted weekends and evenings for two years preparing a feasibility study. Having digested the weighty document, in May 1999 the BAE Systems 'top brass' asked for a meeting.

"They announced that no money would be forthcoming," said Robert, "but it was clear that we should get on with it!" This was a mighty pat on the back for the Vulcan team; they'd got a 'yes' where a 'no' seemed the only likely outcome.

After that, key players like Rolls-Royce came on board. The aero engine giant insisted that the project use zero-timed Olympus turbojets and offered its services. The original equipment manufacturers (OEMs), most having amalgamated or been renamed, also dropped into place. "The aerospace industry has been fantastic. We needed a 100% response – 99% would be a non-starter."

PEOPLE POWER

Having got the 'go' from BAE Systems as the Vulcan's design authority, the engineering phase could accelerate – but with this, the project's limited financial resources would be quickly swallowed up. "We were looking for commercial sponsorship for the restoration and, hopefully, the operation. For a variety of reasons, this was not forthcoming and we needed to harness public support."

In recent years the term 'crowdfunding' has been used to describe this method of finance and the Vulcan to the Sky Trust (VTST) team became masters of the process. This was just as well, as in the very year that XH558 began operating as a civilian – 2008 – the great financial crash ripped through the world economy. "With this, all sponsorship hopes collapsed and, while we have found some great commercial supporters, it has been the unstinting backing of the public that has kept the Vulcan in the air."

The Vulcan to the Sky Club currently has about 5,000 members and its championing of XH558 has been vital to the project. "They are all incredibly loyal and have proved themselves to be helpful in ways we could not have imagined."

As well as crowdfunding, VTST has embraced every element of modern-day communications and social media platforms. During 2015, more than 89,000 e-mail newsletters were shot into cyberspace every time there was an announcement, new fundraisers became available or there were changes of where to see XH558 in action.

CURTAIN CALL

When the Vulcan achieved the only CAA 'complex' category permit to fly, all involved knew it was not an open-ended arrangement — XH558 had a finite flying life, initially set at five years. The agreement with BAE Systems included an undertaking to give 12 months' notice if at all possible; there could be nothing worse than to 'park' the Vulcan for the winter only to discover retrospectively that it had flown its last sortie.

I asked Robert when the certainty dawned that the end was approaching. "It was intimated in 2013, but during the following year we worked to extend through to 2017." In the early weeks of 2015, Marshall Aerospace, as the engineering authority, and BAE Systems, the design authority, acting collectively on behalf of the OEMs, formally brought the arrangement to

a close – XH558 would be retired by the end of the year.

The genesis of restoring the Vulcan to flight lay with design authority being vested in the project – with that endorsement withdrawn there could be no other way to keep going. "We naturally pressed for an extension, but it became obvious that the position was not going to change."

There was no point in protesting; every day beyond the original five years was an incredible bonus. What was needed was to put all the resources and expertise of VTST and the support club into creating the most memorable display season ever and to prepare the way for the already mooted visitor centre at Robin Hood Airport. Everything was put into overdrive to enable the Vulcan to bow out in the finest of styles.

LOWS AND HIGHS

I asked Robert what were the 'lows' of life with the Vulcan. The original rejection by the Heritage Lottery Fund (HLF) was a severe blow, but it was counter-balanced by a barrage of public outcry. This took HLF by surprise and it dawned on the organisation just what a national treasure the Vulcan had become.

The late discovery of corrosion in the undercarriage bay shot the costs up considerably and led to the gut-wrenching prospect of putting the engineering team on notice. Thankfully things did not come to that.

Robert's 'highs' were to do with people. The public and the supporters "have been a constant boost to morale", he said. "Whenever things looked bleak there would be waves of encouragement coming at us."

Even down the phone, the warmth and pride Robert had for the VTST team – be they engineering, technical, administrative or flight crew – was evident. "The team has been brilliant throughout, all helping and supporting one another. Each has exhibited hidden talents; all have remarkable determination."

TO THE FUTURE!

With 18 Vulcan years under his belt, Robert is keen to take a step back, but knows the gravitational pull of XH558 is too strong for him to break away fully. He is looking forward to helping to establish the visitor centre and the academy within the Etna Project at Robin Hood Airport (much more of this on page 78).

He's certainly determined to cut down the long-distance commuting, and wear and tear on his car phone! During his time with the Vulcan, technology has evolved to permit him to work more and more from home – he's looking forward to harnessing that.

Robert is passionate about inspiring youngsters, especially those in the 7 to 14 age group, to take up an interest, and hopefully a career, in technology. He's already a trustee of the Young Engineers educational charity and sees Etna as an innovative way to extend this important work.

"There's so much potential to inspire the adoption of engineering. The Eden Project [in Cornwall] has done so much to open up environmental studies to youth: I can see Etna doing the same for technology."

Robert's attraction to ventures others have not tackled spurs him on with the next phase of XH558's life: "This is very exciting – there's been nothing like it before. We like unique – unique is good".

Below
Hangar 3 at Robin Hood will become the initial hub of the Etna project.

Bottom
Robert and all the VTST team are very proud of the award from the Institution of Mechanical Engineers.
ALL DARREN HARBAR

Life and Times of a Cold War Warrior

A timeline of the Vulcan and its place in aviation and world history

From conception to retirement, Avro's incredible Vulcan spanned just over four decades. Those years brought extraordinary challenges, tensions and achievements. When the type entered its second flying career – as a civilian – the world had become a very different place.

To help put the Vulcan into its historical context, we've chosen a selection of events from both the aviation and the wider world. For the former, we've chosen milestones reached largely in the sphere of strategic bombing and military aviation; although occasionally other areas have been allowed in. Political 'hot spots' and warfare that epitomised the 'Cold War' are the main focus of our attention for global developments. British Prime Ministers, US Presidents and General Secretaries of the Communist Party of the USSR are also mentioned.

History being a highly-personalised and multi-faceted study, we make no apologies for our choice of epochs, events, personalities etc.

Our timeline ends in 1993 – when XH558 touched down at Bruntingthorpe for what seemed like the last entry in the type's history. This special edition of *FlyPast* serves as testament that you should never underestimate a Vulcan.

Above
The V-bombers were designed to take Armageddon to the enemy. View from a Valiant during a British H-bomb test in the Indian Ocean, 1957. KEC

Right
The second prototype Vulcan, VX777, the first to be powered by Bristol Olympus 100s, had its maiden flight in the hands of 'Roly' Falk on September 3, 1953. AVRO-KEC

1946

Mar 5: Winston Churchill, former British Prime Minister, made his famous speech at Fulton, Missouri, USA, in which the term 'Iron Curtain' was used for the first time. US President Harry S Truman mentioned the 'special relationship' between the UK and the USA at the same event. (Clement Atlee – Labour – had become British Prime Minister in July 1945.)

Apr 14: First use of the phrase 'Cold War' in direct reference to relations between the USA and the USSR. An era is defined.

Aug 1: First flight of US Convair B-36 Peacemaker strategic bomber powered by six 'pusher' piston engines.

Dec 17: Operational Requirement OR.229 released for a 100,000lb (45,359kg) medium-range bomber as an Avro Lancaster and Lincoln replacement. Later it was modified to allow the carriage of a 10,000lb 'special' – atomic – weapon 1,724 miles (2,775km).

1947

Jan 7: Specification B35/46 issued to industry for new jet-powered bomber to meet OR.229.

Jul 3: Tupolev Tu-4 *Bull*, a 'reverse-engineered' copy of the B-29 Superfortress, first flown in the USSR.

Jul 28: Tender from Avro for B35/46 accepted by Ministry of Supply and decision taken to proceed. The Avro Type 698 configuration was agreed on November 27, 1947 and on January 1, 1948, issued instructions to proceed.

Dec 17: Boeing B-47 Stratojet six-jet bomber first flown.

1948

Mar 31: Partial blockade of Berlin began and this became complete on June 24.

Jun 25: Berlin Airlift started; supplying the needs of the city by air from West Germany.

Oct 22: Specification E15/48 issued to Avro for low-speed Type 707 and high-speed Type 710 'mini-deltas' to aid Type 698 development. Type 710 was later cancelled as unnecessary.

1949

Apr 4: North Atlantic Treaty Organisation (NATO) established.

May 13: English Electric Canberra jet bomber first flown.

Jul 14: USSR exploded its first atomic weapon.

Sep 4: Avro 707 VX784 first flown from Boscombe Down, Wiltshire, with Flt Lt Eric Esler at the controls. Aircraft and pilot were lost in an accident 27 days later.

Sep 21: Federal Republic of Germany established (ie West Germany).

Oct 1: People's Republic of China declared with Mao Tse Tung (or Mao Zedong in more recent spelling) as leader.

Oct 7: German Democratic Republic set up (ie East Germany).

Above
It was Winston Churchill who coined the phrase 'Iron Curtain' in 1946 as relations between the Soviet Union and the West continued to decay.
PETER GREEN COLLECTION

1950

May 6: First ground run of Bristol BE.10 Olympus powerplant destined for the Avro 698.

Jun 25: Korean War broke out.

Sep 6: First flight of 707B VX790 at Woodford.

Oct 7: China invaded Tibet.

Oct 15: China intervened in the Korean War.

1951

May 18: Vickers Valiant V-bomber prototype first flown.

Oct 26: Winston Churchill (Conservative) elected UK Prime Minister for the second time.

1952

Spring: Prototype Tupolev Type 'N' (or Tu-88) first flown. The production version, the Tu-16 *Badger* strategic bomber, entered service the following year.

Apr 25: The eight-jet Boeing B-52 Stratofortress had its maiden flight in the US.

Aug 14: First production contract issued, for 25 production Avro 698s.

Aug 30: The first prototype Avro 698 VX770, powered by Rolls-Royce Avons, made its first flight at Woodford with 'Roly' Falk at the controls.

Oct 2: Air Council allocated the name Vulcan to the Type 698.

Nov 1: US exploded its first hydrogen bomb.

Nov 6: Dwight D Eisenhower (Republican) became President of the USA.

Dec 24: Handley Page Victor V-bomber first flown.

1953

Mar 5: USSR Premier Joseph Stalin died.

May: First public appearance of the Myasishchev M-4 *Bison* four-jet strategic bomber.

Jul 27: Korean War armistice established.

Aug 20: USSR exploded its first H-bomb.

Sep: Tupolev Tu-20 four-turboprop strategic bomber made its first flight around this time.

Sep 3: Second prototype Vulcan (VX777) powered by Rolls-Royce Olympus 100s made its first flight.

Sep 12: Nikita Khrushchev became First Secretary of the Soviet Communist Party.

1954

May 13: French bastion at Dien Bien Phu, Vietnam, surrendered.

1955

Feb 4: XA889, the first production Vulcan B.1, made its first flight.

Feb 8: First operational Vickers Valiant B.1s issued to 139 Squadron at Gaydon.

Mar: First order for Vulcan B.2s placed.

Apr 5: Anthony Eden (Conservative) became UK Prime Minister.

May 9: West Germany joined NATO.

May 14: Warsaw Pact signed between 'Eastern Bloc' countries.

May 15: USSR pulled its military units out of Austria.

Jun 29: Boeing B-52 Stratofortress entered service with the USAF's Strategic Air Command.

May: Production examples of the Tupolev Tu-95 *Bear* – derived from the Tu-20 – flown at the May Day celebrations.

1956

Mar: 'Blue Danube' free-fall nuclear weapon entered RAF service with the Valiant bomber fleet: it was later carried by the Vulcan.

May 29: Vulcan B.1 cleared for operational service with the RAF after receiving its Controller (Air) Release.

May 31: 230 Operational Conversion Unit (OCU) formed at Waddington, Lincs, to train Vulcan crews. First Vulcan B.1 (XA897) was symbolically handed over to 230 OCU on July 20.

Jul 26: Egypt nationalised the Suez Canal.

Oct 1: XA897 became the first Vulcan B.1 to be lost, crashing at Heathrow Airport at the end of a record-breaking flight to New Zealand and back.

Oct 23: Start of uprising in Hungary.

Oct 29: Israel attacked Egypt; UK and France served ultimatum on Egypt.

Nov 4: USSR intervened in Hungarian uprising; tanks in Budapest.

Nov 5: UK and France invaded the Egyptian Canal Zone – troops withdrawn December 23.

Oct 11: A Valiant of 49 Squadron dropped an atom bomb over Maralinga, South Australia – the first RAF aircraft to do so. Nov 11: Convair XB-58 Hustler four-jet supersonic bomber first flown.

1957

Jan 9: Harold Macmillan (Conservative) became UK Prime Minister.

Feb 19: Training of initial intake of Vulcan aircrews begins at 230 OCU.

May 15: A Valiant of 49 Squadron dropped an H-bomb over Christmas Island, Pacific – the first RAF aircraft to do so.

Jul 11: First Vulcan B.1s delivered to 83 Squadron at Waddington – the type's first operational unit.

Aug 26: USSR tested its first Intercontinental Ballistic Missile (ICBM).

Oct 4: USSR launched *Sputnik*, the world's first artificial satellite, from the Baikonur Cosmodrome. The launch vehicle was a modified ICBM – the 'Cold War' ramped up considerably from this day.

1958

Feb 1: *Explorer 1*, the first US satellite, launched by a Jupiter-C – derived from an ICBM – from Cape Canaveral, Florida.

Mar: 'Violet Club' nuclear weapon entered service for Valiants and Vulcans.

Jul: Each V-bomber station was expected to have 20% of its aircraft ready to launch within two hours of a Strategic Warning, increasing to 40, 60 and 75% within four, eight and 24 hours from this month.

Aug 19: First production Vulcan B.2 (XH533) flown.

Oct: US nuclear weapons, including the free-fall Mk.5, arrived to arm Bomber Command.

1959

Jan 1: Fidel Castro declared victory in Cuba – a Communist-based state had been established on the USA's 'doorstep'.

Feb 12: Last USAF Convair B-36 Peacemaker withdrawn from frontline service with USAF.

Jul: Start of conversion programme to upgrade Vulcan B.1s with electronic countermeasures as B.1As. First B.1A entered service with 617 Squadron on September 30.

Above
Aircrew boarding a 15 Squadron Victor B.1 at Cottesmore 1959. ARMSTRONG SIDDELEY

Below
Boeing's incredible eight-engined B-52 Stratofortress first flew in 1952 and entered service with Strategic Air Command three years later. Incredibly, B-52s are still in frontline service with the USAF. BOEING

1960

Mar: US Government agreed to supply Douglas AGM-87A Skybolt air-launched ballistic missiles to the UK for the Vulcan.

May: Vulcan B.2 cleared for operational RAF service.

May 5: The USSR shot down a US Lockheed U-2 'spyplane' over Sverdlovsk and captured its pilot, Gary Powers.

Jul 1: First Vulcan B.1 (XH533) was delivered to 'B' Flight of 230 OCU at Waddington.

Sep: 'Violet Club' nuclear weapons carried by Vulcans at Finningley and Scampton replaced by 'Yellow Sun'.

Nov 7: John F Kennedy (Democrat) became President of the USA.

1961

Apr 12: Yuri Gagarin of the USSR became the first man in space; he was up for 108 minutes including one orbit of the planet.

Apr 17: 'Bay of Pigs' landing in Cuba by US-backed dissidents; in an abortive attempt to overthrow Castro.

May: Tupolev's twin-jet supersonic strategic bomber, the Tu-22 *Blinder,* had its public debut – first flight very likely took place in 1959.

May 5: Alan B Shepard became first American in space, with a 15-minute sortie in the Mercury capsule *Freedom 7.*

Jun 3: Khrushchev and Kennedy met in Vienna, Austria.

Aug 13-19: 'Berlin Wall' erected.

Dec: USA dramatically increased number of 'advisers' in South Vietnam; start of major US involvement.

1962

Jan 1: A 15-minute Quick Reaction Alert was initiated by each Vulcan squadron.

May: Vulcan tactics changed to include low-level penetration of the Soviet Union.

Jun 20: Telephone 'hot-line' is established between Washington and Moscow.

Aug 5: UK, USA and USSR signed partial nuclear test ban treaty.

Oct 18: Sir Alec Douglas-Home (Conservative) became UK Prime Minister.

Nov 22: President Kennedy assassinated; Lyndon B Johnson (Democrat) became President of the USA.

1964

Apr: White 'anti-flash' scheme replaced by a camouflage pattern effective at low-level for V-bombers.

Feb: Valiant retired from RAF service.

Feb 7: US began bombing raids on North Vietnam.

Jul: General Dynamics terrain-following radar ordered for the V-force. Vulcan B.2s were distinguished by a 'thimble' radome on the nose.

Aug 25: Indo-Pakistan war started – peace talks began in January 1966.

1966

Feb: Last B-47 Stratojets withdrawn from USAF service.

Mar 7: France withdrew from NATO.

Apr 18: China started the so-called 'Cultural Revolution'.

Left
The Soviet Union persisted with turboprops for some of its strategic bomber fleet - Tupolev Tu-95 'Bear', 1992.
KEY-DUNCAN CUBITT

Feb 20: *Friendship 7*, a Mercury capsule, put John H Glenn into Earth orbit from an Atlas ICBM booster; the first American in orbit.

Jul 10: *Telstar* communications satellite launched by a Delta rocket – TV programmes were beamed across the planet.

Sep: Avro 'Blue Steel' air-to-surface missile entered interim operational RAF service with 617 Squadron.

Oct 18: US Lockheed U-2 spotted USSR Intermediate Range Ballistic Missiles (IRBMs) being set up in Cuba.

Oct 22: US imposed a 'quarantine' of Cuba – crisis at its height.

Oct 28: USSR announced withdrawal of IRBMs from Cuba alongside secret agreement from USA to remove IRBMs from Turkey.

Dec 21: Skybolt missile system cancelled.

1963

Jan: V-bomber force integrated within NATO's nuclear strike plans. Operational Readiness Platforms were built at the end of the runways at Vulcan bases in preparation for the 'four-minute warning' of detection of a Soviet missile launch.

Feb: Full operational clearance with 'Blue Steel' achieved.

Mar 6: Last of the 28 Vulcan B.1As re-delivered to Waddington.

Sep 21: North American XB-70A Valkyrie Mach 3 strategic bomber first flown for research purposes only; the programme having been terminated as a bomber prior to its maiden flight.

Sep 27: BAC TSR.2 made its first flight. The programme was cancelled on April 6, 1965.

Oct 15: Leonid Brezhnev became General Secretary of the Communist Party of the USSR.

Oct 16: People's Republic of China exploded its first atomic weapon. Harold Wilson (Labour) became UK Prime Minister.

1965

Jan 15: Last Vulcan B.2 (XM657) delivered to the RAF.

Sep: WE177B nuclear weapon cleared for use on Vulcan force.

Dec: Twin-engined supersonic strategic bomber, the Tupolev Tu-22M *Backfire*, believed to have started development flying.

1967

Jun 5-9: Six-Day War in the Middle East; Israel attacked Egypt, Jordan and Syria.

Jun 17: China tested first H-bomb and on August 24 so did France.

Jul 30: Bomber version of the twin-jet 'swing-wing' General Dynamics F-111, the FB-111A, first flown; entering service in August 1969.

Dec 31: 12 Squadron at Cottesmore became the first Vulcan unit to disband.

Above
Convair's awesome B-58 Hustler, without the under-fuselage bomb and fuel pod, at Edwards Air Force Base in October 1961. USAF-KEC

1968

Jan 10: Last pair of Vulcan B.1As retired from operational duties.

Apr 30: Bomber Command replaced by Strike Command.

Aug 21: USSR invaded Czechoslovakia.

Nov 1: US stopped bombing of North Vietnam – but see 1972!

Right
While sharing the designation Tu-22 with the 'Blinder', the swing-wing Tu-22M 'Backfire' was an entirely new design, having its debut in 1966. KEY-DUNCAN CUBITT

1969

Jan 20: Richard M Nixon (Republican) became President of the USA.

Feb 9: First flight of the Boeing 747 'Jumbojet' prototype, Seattle, USA.

Above
A Tupolev Tu-22UB trainer variant taking off in 1992. The first example of this twin-engined strategic bomber probably first flew in 1959.
KEY-DUNCAN CUBITT

Mar 2: The Anglo-French BAC/SNIAS Concorde supersonic airliner had its maiden flight, from Toulouse, France. The design was powered by versions of the Vulcan's Olympus turbojets. The first UK-completed machine flew from Filton, Bristol on Apr 9. (Concorde had been 'pipped at the post' by the Soviet Union. On December 31, 1968, it first flew the Tupolev Tu-144 supersonic airliner, USSR.) Also on this day major border clashes broke out between China and USSR.

Jun 30: Royal Navy Polaris submarine fleet assumed nuclear deterrent role from V-bomber force.

Jul 16-24: *Apollo 11* took man to the Moon and back – Neil A Armstrong, Edwin E A Aldrin and Michael Collins. Armstrong became the first man on the Moon on the 21st.

1970

Jun: Last B-58 Hustlers withdrawn from USAF service.

Jun 19: Edward Heath (Conservative) became UK Prime Minister.

Dec 21: 617 Squadron flew the last sortie carrying 'Blue Steel'.

1972

May 26: Strategic Arms Limitation Treaty signed by USA and USSR.

Dec 29: Last major bombing of North Vietnam by US.

1973

Oct 6-26: Yom Kippur ('Day of Atonement') War broke out in the Middle East; Egypt, Syria, Jordan and Iraq struck at Israel.

1974

Jan 15: US stopped offensive military actions in Vietnam; cease-fire came into effect on the 27th. The following year, the hasty evacuation of Saigon was carried out by helicopters, ending on April 30, 1975.

Aug 9: Gerald R Ford (Republican) became President of the USA.

Oct 11: Harold Wilson (Labour) became UK Prime Minister for the second time.

Dec 23: Rockwell B-1 swing-wing, supersonic strategic bomber first flown - programme put on ice in 1977.

1976

Mar 16: James Callaghan (Labour) was elected UK Prime Minister.

1977

Jan 20: James E Carter (Democrat) became President of the USA.

1979

Feb 22: XA903 makes the last flight of a Vulcan B.1, landing at Farnborough.

May 4: Margaret Thatcher (Conservative) became UK Prime Minister.

Dec 24: The USSR invaded Afghanistan and began a decade of bloody conflict, unresolved by the time of its pull-out in 1989.

1981

First flight of the Tupolev Tu-160 *Blackjack* swing-wing, supersonic strategic bomber, USSR, at some time during the year.

Jan 20: Ronald W Reagan (Republican) became President of the USA.

1982

Mar 30: 27 Squadron disbanded, ending Vulcan operations at Scampton.

Apr 2: Falkland Islands occupied by Argentinean forces. Vulcan units prepared for sorties in support of Operation 'Corporate'.

Apr 29: First two Vulcans departed Waddington for Wideawake, Ascension Island. No.9 Squadron disbanded at Waddington.

Apr 30: First Vulcan delivered to Woodford for conversion as K.2 tanker. Flt Lt Martin Withers and his crew in XM607 took off from Ascension Island as *Black Buck 1* – the longest bombing raid undertaken by the RAF at the time, with a flight time of 15 hours 45 minutes. This was the Vulcan's combat debut.

May 2: Argentine Navy cruiser *General Belgrano* sunk by the Royal Navy nuclear submarine *Conqueror*.

May 3: XM607 embarked on *Black Buck 2*, a repeat of the earlier raid.

May 5: Test firing of AS37 Martel air-to-ground missiles carried on pylons under XM597 were carried out over the range at Aberporth, Wales. This was the conclusion of a hasty programme that enabled the RAF to counter Argentine radars in the Falklands. Low stocks of Martels resulted in replacement by Texas Instruments AGM-45A Shrikes.

May 16: *Black Buck 4* raid cancelled.

May 28: First raid with Shrikes, *Black Buck 4*, launched but abandoned when a

hose on one of the Victor tankers broke. May 30: *Black Buck 5* achieved the first operational launch of Shrikes from Vulcan XM597.

Jun 2: XM597 destroyed a radar with a pair of Shrikes during *Black Buck 6*. Heading back to Wideawake the Vulcan's probe broke, ending fuel transfer and forcing the crew to divert to Rio de Janeiro in Brazil, where the aircraft was impounded for eight days.

Jun 11: Final operational raid launched. *Black Buck 7* delivered air-burst bombs over Port Stanley.

Jun 14: Vulcans returned from Ascension Island after the Argentinean forces on the Falkland Islands surrendered.

Jun 18: Vulcan K.2 XH561 made the maiden flight of the tanker variant. Five days later Controller (Aircraft) release was gained for K.2, allowing it to enter service with 50 Squadron.

Nov 12: Yuri V Andropov became General Secretary of the Communist Party of the USSR.

Above
Seen as a Canberra replacement, on the first prototype BAC TSR.2, XR219, took to the skies before the entire programme was axed. BAC-KEC

Below left
The first of two North American XB-70A Valkyries, 62-0001, is preserved at the National Museum of the USAF at Dayton, Ohio. KEY-STEVE FLETCHER

Dec 17: Four Vulcan B.2s (XL391, XM597, XM607 and XM612) undertook a last, 'farewell' flypast of former bases.

Dec 22: The Vulcan left RAF service in the bomber role when 44 Squadron disbanded at Waddington.

1983

Mar 23: US President Reagan announced the Strategic Defense Initiative – immediately referred to as 'Star Wars'. This high-tech global defence system was never put into operation.

1984

Feb 9: Konstantin Chernenko became General Secretary of the Communist Party of the USSR.

Mar 31: Disbandment of 50 Squadron ended the Vulcan's operational service career, although two were retained as display aircraft.

1985

Mar 11: Mikhail S Gorbachev became General Secretary of the Communist Party of the USSR.

Oct 18: Rockwell B-1B Lancer prototype first flown, USA. (The B-1 programme had been cancelled by President Carter in 1977; but was resurrected by President Reagan in 1981.)

1986

Mar: XA900, the last complete Vulcan B.1, was scrapped at Cosford.

Apr 26: Chernobyl nuclear powerplant disaster.

May 10: Boeing B-52H Stratofortresses became operational with Boeing AGM-86 cruise missiles.

Dec 19: One of the last two display aircraft, XL426, made its final flight, to preservation a Southend.

1988

Dec 21: PanAm flight PA103 downed by a terrorist bomb on a flight from London to New York; crashing at Lockerbie, Scotland.

1989

Jan 20: George H W Bush (Republican) became President of the USA.

Jun 3-4: Massacre of protesting students and others, Tiananmen Square, Beijing, China.

Jul 17: Northrop B-2 'stealth' bomber was first flown – it was later named Spirit.

Nov 9: The 'Berlin Wall' was no longer a 'hard' border, free access was allowed in either direction and quickly the wall sections were demolished by excited members of the German public.

Dec 25: Romanian Premier Nicolae Ceaucescu and his wife were executed.

1990

Mar 15: Mikhail S Gorbachev (previously General Secretary of the Communist Party) became first and last President of the Soviet Union; presiding over its dissolution.

Aug 2: Iraqi forces invaded Kuwait.

Oct 3: East and West Germany reunified.

Nov 22: John Major (Conservative) elected UK Prime Minister.

1991

Jan 17: Coalition forces, led by the USA, launched Operation 'Desert Storm', the Liberation of Kuwait.

Feb 28: Hostilities come to an end in Gulf War.

Jul 10: Boris Yeltsin became the first President of the Russian Federation.

Dec 25: USSR officially dissolved.

1992

Sep 20: Last RAF Vulcan display performed at Cranfield, by XH558.

Sep 21: Vulcan Display Flight disbanded at Waddington.

Oct: Last FB-111s withdrawn from USAF service.

1993

Jan 20: William J Clinton (Democrat) became President of the USA.

Mar 23: Last airworthy Vulcan (XH558) delivered to Bruntingthorpe, Leicestershire, on its final flight – or so it seemed!

Oct 1993: Last of the Victor K.2 fleet retired.

Timeline compiled with many thanks to Dave Willis.

Below left
First flown in 1974, axed in 1977 and re-activated in 1985, Rockwell B-1B Lancers are still in service.
KEY-DUNCAN CUBITT

Below
The 'stealth' bomber, the Northrop B-2 Spirit, has been around since 1989 and its small fleet is still at the forefront of USAF strategic thinking.
KEY-MARK NICHOLLS

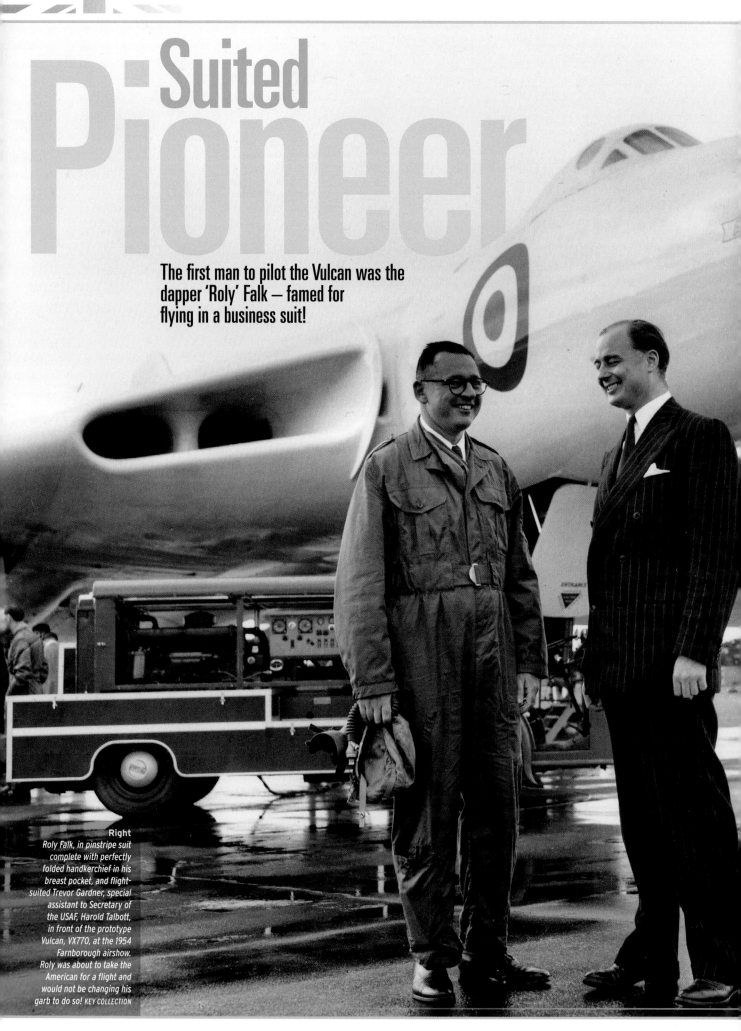

Suited Pioneer

The first man to pilot the Vulcan was the dapper 'Roly' Falk — famed for flying in a business suit!

Right
Roly Falk, in pinstripe suit complete with perfectly folded handkerchief in his breast pocket, and flight-suited Trevor Gardner, special assistant to Secretary of the USAF, Harold Talbott, in front of the prototype Vulcan, VX770, at the 1954 Farnborough airshow. Roly was about to take the American for a flight and would not be changing his garb to do so! KEY COLLECTION

Above
The prototype Vulcan, VX770, powered by Rolls-Royce Avons.
HAWKER SIDDELEY-KEY

R oland John Falk could not have asked for a better start to a career in aviation. He studied at the de Havilland Technical School, Hatfield, and learned to fly there, aged 17, in 1932. In June 1935 he briefly joined Air Commerce at Croydon before working on a freelance basis for Air Dispatch, also based at Croydon, and its associate business, Commercial Air Hire (CAH) of Heston.

Air Dispatch had contracts to fly newspapers to and from the Continent, including Madrid and Paris, as well as charter work, mostly using Airspeed Envoys. The small set-up specialised in flying film crews, news reporters, film reels and high-value packages. 'Roly' flew press representatives to Abyssinia (now Ethiopia) during the Italian invasion in October 1935, returning in early December.

In 1936 he found himself amid another conflict, the Spanish Civil War, and on July 21 flew three journalists in Envoy G-ADAZ to Barajas, Madrid, then in the hands of republican forces. Four days later, he had four passengers and two resident Air Dispatch staff to extract, but was lacking the necessary paperwork. Roly bluffed his way through, but was pursued by fighters as he headed for the French border. Thankfully the 170mph (273km/h) Envoy was more than a match for its followers.

The following February he became a test pilot for the Air Registration Board on an 'as and when' basis (the ARB was the precursor of the Civil Aviation Authority).

In February 1940 Roly joined the RAF and was posted to the Royal Aircraft Establishment (RAE) at Farnborough. His flying skills were such that in 1943 he succeeded Wg Cdr H J Wilson as the RAE's chief test pilot (CTP), flying a staggering 300 different types and around 2,000 hours during his time at Farnborough.

"THE WELLINGTON'S NOSE DIPPED VIOLENTLY DOWNWARDS AND ROLY BECAME A PASSENGER; IT PLOUGHED THROUGH THE FARMHOUSE.... AND CAME TO REST IN A BALL OF FLAME ON A MINOR ROAD."

MINI VULCANS - THE 707S

The airframe concept for the Avro Type 698 required as much data as possible before the full-scale prototype undertook its first flight. One answer to this pressing need was a series of small delta-wing research aircraft, in order that the aerodynamic properties be better assessed. The first of five Type 707s, all powered by Rolls-Royce Derwents, was short-lived. Flying from Boscombe Down, VX784 first flew on September 4, 1949, piloted by S E 'Red' Esler. After an appearance at that year's Farnborough Airshow it crashed on September 30, killing Esler.

The second aircraft, 707B VX790, was, like the original 707, fitted with a dorsal intake for the engine. It first flew on September 6, 1950, from Boscombe Down, piloted by 'Roly' Falk. The third aircraft was 707A WD280, which was the first with engine intakes in the wing roots and therefore had a layout very similar to the Vulcan's. This first flew on June 14, 1951 and was eventually shipped to Australia for further trials. It is now privately owned in Melbourne.

Assembled at the Avro facility at Bracebridge Heath, Lincolnshire, and tested from adjacent Waddington airfield, Avro 707A WZ736 first flew on February 20, 1953, and was not ordered specifically for the Vulcan programme but for delta research by the Royal Aircraft Establishment. Retired in 1967 after auto-throttle trials, WZ736 is now on show at the Museum of Science and Industry, Manchester.

A batch of four Avro 707Cs was also ordered, but in the end only WZ744 was completed, again at Bracebridge Heath, with first flight at Waddington on July 1, 1953. The 707C was a two-seat, side-by-side trainer which the RAF envisaged would help transition to the Vulcan - but, as it turned out, such a step-up was not needed. It later flew from the RAE at Bedford on high-speed trials work and with an early form of fly-by-wire control (in duplicated form). It is on show at the RAF Museum, Cosford.

> "...THE FIRST 707 HAD LESS THAN THREE HOURS 'ON THE CLOCK' WHEN IT WAS LOST, SO HAD NOT BEGUN TO CONTRIBUTE AERODYNAMIC EXPERIENCE OR DATA TO THE VULCAN PROGRAMME."

Avro 707A WD280, first flown by Roly Falk on June 14, 1951. AVRO-PETER GREEN COLLECTION

fitted with reversible pitch propellers. They were intended to help shorten the landing run, but there was a belief that they may well be able to help decelerate the new airliner on approach. Roly was tasked with trying this out.

Flying solo on July 5, 1946, he took LN817 up for a circuit, engaging the reverse pitch about half-a-mile from the threshold. The Wellington's nose dipped violently downwards and Roly became a passenger; the aircraft ploughed through the farmhouse at Cuckoo Farm, near Ockham, and came to rest in a ball of flame on a minor road.

Roly had been thrown clear. He had broken both legs and an arm and had a spinal fracture. He faced a long time in hospital and then recuperation and his job with Vickers came to an end. It was determined that the prop pitch control mechanism on LN817 malfunctioned, causing a violent pitch-down on approach.

Right Classic departure from Farnborough: Roly Falk tucking up the gear on the second prototype Vulcan, VX777. KEC

He piloted a wide range of captured Luftwaffe types, including the Heinkel He 162A, Messerschmitt Bf 109G, Bf 110C, Me 163B rocket fighter (as a glider only), Me 262B twin-jet, Focke-Wulf Fw 190A and a variety of Junkers Ju 88s.

ERRANT WELLINGTON

Wing Commander Roland Falk AFC* joined Vickers at Brooklands in January 1946 – working for its CTP, 'Mutt' Summers – initially testing Viking airliners. As part of the programme leading up to the Viscount four-turboprop airliner, Wellington B.X LN817 had been

MINI-DELTA

Against all the odds, by April 1947 Roly was up and flying, reverting to the role of a charter pilot. On September 30, 1949 Avro test pilot S E 'Red' Esler was killed in the prototype 707 delta test-bed (see the panel) and in January 1950 Roly joined Avro at Woodford under CTP 'Jimmy' Orrell.

Effectively, Roly was project pilot for the 707 and the programme that dominated all others at Woodford, the Avro 698 V-bomber, which took the name Vulcan in December 1952. Such was his level of experience that his appointment was ratified in the spring of 1954 as Superintendent of Flying, instead of the more usual Deputy CTP.

The first 707 had less than three hours 'on the clock' when it was lost, so had not begun to contribute aerodynamic experience or data to the

Vulcan programme. While it appeared that the delta configuration did not contribute to VX784's demise, no real cause could be attributed.

The second mini-delta, the 707B, featured many design changes and an ejection seat; Roly took VX790 into the air for its maiden flight on September 6, 1950. The following year the much refined 707A (which dispensed with the single upper-fuselage intake of the first two examples and adopted wing root intakes to emulate the format of the Vulcan) made its debut in Roy's hands. Two more 707s followed, both after the first flight of the prototype Vulcan.

VULCAN DEBUT

Roly flew the prototype Vulcan, VX770, solo from Woodford on August 30, 1952 for 36 minutes. Flying on his own was not bravado, nor a reflection of how fearful he and Avro were of the time: VX770 was in interim condition; its Bristol Siddeley Olympus engines were not ready so Rolls-Royce Avons were fitted and there was no second seat for a co-pilot. The sortie was a great success, the only 'wobble' occurring on landing back at Woodford when two main undercarriage doors fell off.

Operating from Boscombe Down, Roly and VX770 stunned the airshow audience at Farnborough in the first week of September, flying in formation with 707A WD280 and 707B VX790.

A year later, Roly was in command of the second prototype, VX777, for its debut. It had Olympus 100s and took on the bulk of the development flying. For the 1953 Farnborough show Avro wanted to increase the 'wow factor' still further, especially

as the rival prototype Handley Page Victor was also in attendance. Flying VX777, Roly was 'escorted' by 707As WD280, WZ736, 707B VX790 and 707C WZ744 before he started his solo display, which included slow-rolling the big delta.

While showing an RAE crew the Vulcan's slow flying characteristics in VX777 at Farnborough on July 27, 1954 a control spring in the rudder jammed and Roly found himself with a full deflection on the rudder while the pedals were centred. He returned to Farnborough, made a fast approach and overran, the delta ending up on its belly but with only minor injuries to the crew. The precious prototype was back in the air the following March.

Trials proved that the 'pure' delta needed modification and in July 1955 Roly piloted VX777 with a distinctive 'kink' on the outer leading edge, the so-called Phase 2 wing. With the retirement of Jimmy Orrell in 1955, Roly became Avro CTP in August 1957.

Wg Cdr Roland John Falk OBE AFC* retired from flying in January 1958, taking up a role as a sales representative for the Americas with Hawker Siddeley. His place at Woodford was taken by 'Jimmy' Harrison.

In 1963 Roly began working as a freelance consultant before settling in Jersey in 1967 to run his own charter business. He died on the island on February 23, 1985, aged 69.

Adapted from Volume One of Testing to the Limits – British Test Pilots since 1910, *by Ken Ellis, from Crécy Publishing, priced at £24.95. Volume Two will be published in early spring 2016.* **www.crecy.co.uk**

Fore and aft

Inside XH558's cockpit

Take a look inside of cockpit of XH558 in the last year of its operation with the Vulcan Display Flight, 1992. There was generally a five-strong crew in operational Vulcans: captain, co-pilot, navigator and two air electronics officers (AEO) - the latter three flew backwards into battle!

Occasionally there would be a sixth occupant, normally the crew chief, sometimes a 'high-ranker', guest or an examiner; rarely a weapons specialist. Occupying the AEO's bench is Sqn Ldr Barry Masefield,

a great supporter of XH558 and he was on board during its first test flight as a civilian on October 18, 2007 and was part of the VTST flight crew until 2013.

Barry started in the RAF with a radar technician apprenticeship in 1959. Four years later he was selected for aircrew as an AEO and for the next 17 years flew on Shackletons and Nimrods. Commissioned in 1979, Barry moved to Vulcans, first with 230 OCU, then 617 and 50 Squadrons. Barry was selected for the 'Black Buck' sorties to the Falkland

Islands during his time with 50, and was AEO for the second raid.

After the conflict ended, Barry flew with 44 Squadron until it disbanded. He then joined the Victor K.2 tanker fleet as an AEO. One war was not enough for Barry; he was part of the Victor Force serving in the first Gulf War in 1993 before retiring from 'The Firm'. While at Marham with the Victors, he flew as AEO with the Vulcan Display Flight and was part of the crew on XH558's 'final' sortie, to Bruntingthorpe, on March 23, 1993. ◉

BOTH KEY-DUNCANCUBITT

VULCAN

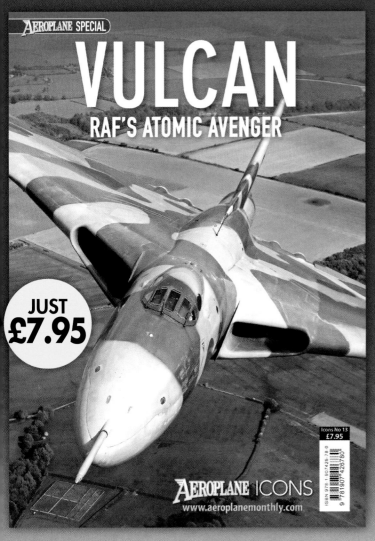

AEROPLANE SPECIAL

VULCAN
RAF'S ATOMIC AVENGER

JUST
£7.95

Icons No 13
£7.95

AEROPLANE ICONS
www.aeroplanemonthly.com

ISBN 978-1-907426-78-0

The RAF's Atomic Avenger

The Aeroplane ICONS series celebrates the history of aviation. Exploring and illustrating the history of iconic aircraft from around the world. Highlighting some of the great aircraft, this series is the perfect read for aviation enthusiasts looking to explore the in-depth history behind these iconic aeroplanes.

Issue 13 - VULCAN
The RAF's Atomic Avenger

OUT NOW

FEATURES INCLUDE:

ATOMIC ACCESSION
The story of Britain's Bomb and the development of atomic

GERMAN GENISIS
The creation of the RAF's nuclear V-Force

DESIGNS AND DIMINUTIVES
Designing the Avro 698- and the Avro 707 series.

DELTA DEVELOPMENTS
Development of the bigger and better Vulcan Mk.2

FALKLANDS FINALE
Conflict over the South Atlantic and the Vulcan's swansong.

AND MUCH MORE!

ORDER DIRECT

JUST £7.95 + FREE P&P*

*Free 2nd class P&P on all UK & BFPO orders. Overseas charges apply.

ALSO AVAILABLE IN DIGITAL FORMAT:

DOWNLOAD NOW

FREE APP
with sample issue
IN APP ISSUES £6.99

SEARCH AEROPLANE ICONS

AVAILABLE FROM:

Available on
BlackBerry

Available on
kindle fire

Available on
PC, Mac &
Windows 8

Available on
iTunes

Available on the
App Store

Available on
Google play

1188/15

Available on PC, Mac, Blackberry, Windows 8 and kindle fire from **pocket**mags.com

Delta
Weaponry

A portfolio of the Vulcan B.2's arsenal

Above
A 'Yellow Sun' free-fall nuclear weapon alongside Valiant BK.1 XD818 at the National Cold War Exhibition at the RAF Museum, Cosford. During its time as the spearhead of the UK's nuclear deterrent, V-force carried a series of such bombs; 'Yellow Sun' was introduced to the Vulcans from 1960. *KEY-STEVE FLETCHER*

Left
Scampton-based 617 Squadron was the first RAF unit to achieve operational status with the Avro 'Blue Steel' stand-off weapon, from June 1962. The missile had a range of 200 miles, could be launched at high or low level and flew at around Mach 2 to deliver a one-megaton warhead. *KEY COLLECTION*

Far left
The Vulcan's capacious bomb bay could carry 21 'thousand-pounder' conventional bombs. During the Falklands conflict, the Vulcan got to achieve this role for real. *KEC*

From 1960 it was decided that the Vulcan would be equipped with the Douglas AGM-87 Skybolt air-launched ballistic missile, one under each wing. B.2 XH537 flew with dummy missiles at Boscombe Down from March 1961. Although the project was cancelled in 1962, the hardpoints fitted to some of the fleet were to prove vital in the Falklands conflict. *AVRO-KEC*

Under air test, probably from Boscombe Down in May 1982, XM597 carrying a Texas Instruments AGM-45 Shrike anti-radiation missile to port and an ALQ-101 electronic countermeasures pod to starboard. PETER GREEN COLLECTION

Left
In readiness for potential use during the Falklands conflict, trials of the fitment of Matra/HSA AS.37 Martel missiles for the Vulcan began at Waddington on May 5, 1982, although the US-made Shrike was later used for the 'Black Buck' sorties. PETER GREEN COLLECTION

Below left
The 35-foot 'Blue Steel' missile was carried semi-recessed in the Vulcan's bomb bay. The weapon's ventral fin folded to port for ease of loading and clearance on take-off.
KEY COLLECTION

Below
As well as the maritime radar reconnaissance role adopted from 1972, the Vulcan B.2(MRRs of 50 Squadron also carried out high-altitude air sampling sorties. For this purpose underwing pods, modified from DH Sea Vixen drop tanks, were fitted.
KEY-GORDON SWANBOROUGH COLLECTION

A view, looking forward, of XH558's bomb bay during engineering assessment at Bruntingthorpe in November 1999. The bomb doors still carry the giant 'FAREWELL' lettering from its final season as an RAF display aircraft, seven years earlier.. KEY-STEVE FLETCHER

Delta Heraldry

Charting Vulcan B.2 units and markings

Markings are not necessarily to be taken at face value: Vulcan K.2 XM571 carrying the emblem of 101 Squadron on its fin. Such was the pace of the tanker programme that XM571 was taken out of service with 101 in July 1982 and was still wearing its former unit's symbol when it entered flight test in its new role. It was issued to 50 Squadron in October 1982. BRITISH AEROSPACE

B.2 XH557 carrying the bat and Roman numerals 'IX' of 9 Squadron, along with the Waddington Wing badge. PETE WEST © 2015

Issued to 12 Squadron at Coningsby straight from the production line in August 1963, B.2 XM597 wearing the unit's fox head. PETE WEST © 2015

9 SQUADRON

Badge:	A bat
Motto:	Per noctum volamus – Through the night we fly
Previously flew:	English Electric Canberra B.6s to 1961
Mar 1, 1962	Re-formed at Coningsby, Lincs, on Vulcan B.2s
Nov 10, 1964	To Cottesmore, Rutland
Feb 26, 1969	To Akrotiri, Cyprus
Jan 15, 1975	To Waddington, Lincs
May 1, 1982	Disbanded
Post-Vulcan:	Re-formed on Panavia Tornado GR.1s 1982; presently flying Tornado GR.4s as part of the Marham Tornado Wing, Norfolk

12 SQUADRON

Badge:	A fox's mask (ie stylised head)
Motto:	Leads the field
Previously flew:	English Electric Canberra B.6s to 1961
Jul 1, 1962	Re-formed at Coningsby, Lincs, on Vulcan B.2s
Nov 17, 1964	To Cottesmore, Rutland
Dec 31, 1967	Disbanded
Post-Vulcan:	Re-formed on HS Buccaneer S.2s 1969; presently flying Panavia Tornado GR.4s as part of the Marham Tornado Wing, Norfolk

50 SQUADRON

Badge:	A sword in bend severing a mantle, palewise. (A sword cutting a cloak.) On the Vulcans, a pair of stylised greyhounds were used.
Motto:	From defence to attack
Previously flew:	English Electric Canberra B.2s to 1959
Aug 1, 1961	Re-formed at Waddington, Lincs, on Vulcan B.1s
Jan 1966	First Vulcan B.2s arrive
Jun 1982	First Vulcan K.2s arrive
Mar 31, 1984	Disbanded

Vulcan XH558 in K.2 tanker guise in 1983 wearing the greyhound markings of 50 Squadron. *KEC*

44 SQUADRON

Badge:	An elephant, on a mount - has also used a stylised '44'
Motto:	Fulmina regis justa - The King's thunderbolts are righteous
Previously flew:	English Electric Canberra B.2s to 1957
Aug 10, 1960	Re-formed at Waddington, Lincs, on Vulcan B.1s
Sep 1966	First Vulcan B.2s arrive
Dec 21, 1982	Disbanded

Display airframe at Waddington since January 1983, B.2 XM607 in the static at a Battle of Britain 'At Home' day in September 1978, carrying the markings of 44 Squadron. *KEC*

Preserved at Carlisle Airport, XJ823 wearing the Disney character 'Dumbo' on the fin, a variation on 27 Squadron's elephant badge. *KEY-DUNCAN CUBITT*

B.2 XH562 was first issued to 35 Squadron at Scampton in March 1963 and carried the unit's winged horse's head on the fin. *PETE WEST © 2015*

27 SQUADRON

Badge:	An elephant - variations include the Disney character 'Dumbo'
Motto:	Quam celerrime ad astra - With all speed to the stars
Previously flew:	English Electric Canberra B.2s to 1957
Apr 1, 1961	Re-formed at Scampton, Lincs, on Vulcan B.2s
Mar 29, 1972	Disbanded
Nov 1, 1972	Re-formed at Scampton, Lincs, on Vulcan B.2(MRR)s
Mar 31, 1982	Disbanded
Post-Vulcan:	Re-formed on Panavia Tornado GR.1s 1983; presently flying Boeing Chinook HC.2s, 3s, 4s and 6s as part of the Odiham Wing, Joint Helicopter Command, Hampshire

35 SQUADRON

Badge:	A horse's head, winged - has also used a stylised '35'
Motto:	Uno animo agimus - We act with one accord
Previously flew:	English Electric Canberra B.2s to 1961
Dec 1, 1962	Re-formed at Coningsby, Lincs, on Vulcan B.2s
Nov 2, 1964	To Cottesmore, Rutland
Jan 1, 1969	To Akrotiri, Cyprus
Jan 16, 1975	To Scampton, Lincs
Mar 1, 1982	Disbanded

83 SQUADRON

Badge:	An attire. (The antlers of a mature male deer)
Motto:	Strike to defend
Previously flew:	Avro Lincoln B.2s to 1956
May 21, 1957	Re-formed at Waddington, Lincs, on Vulcan B.1s
Oct 10, 1960	To Scampton, Lincs
Dec 1960	First Vulcan B.2s arrive
Aug 31, 1969	Disbanded

The antlers of 83 Squadron on the unit badge. The motto well sums up the Vulcan's deterrent role - 'Strike to Defend'.
KEY COLLECTION

101 SQUADRON

Badge:	Issuant from the battlements of a tower, a demi-lion, guardant. (A lion atop a castle tower.) Has also used a stylised '101'
Motto:	Mens agitat molem - Mind over matter
Previously flew:	English Electric Canberra B.6s to 1957
Oct 15, 1957	Re-formed at Finningley, Yorks, on Vulcan B.1s
Jun 26, 1961	To Waddington, Lincs
Dec 1967	First Vulcan B.2s arrive
Aug 4, 1982	Disbanded
Post-Vulcan:	Re-formed on Vickers VC-10s 1984; presently flying Airbus Voyager KC.2s and KC.3s from Brize Norton, Oxfordshire

230 OPERATIONAL CONVERSION UNIT

Badge:	Sword amid waves - also adopted the white rose of Yorkshire
Previously flew:	Avro Lincoln B.2s to 1955
May 31, 1956	Re-formed at Waddington, on Vulcan B.1s
Jul 1960	First Vulcan B.2s arrive
Jun 18, 1961	To Finningley, Yorks
Dec 8, 1969	To Scampton, Lincs
Aug 31, 1981	Disbanded

VULCAN WINGS

Centralised servicing meant that individual aircraft were nominally hosted by Wings, as follows:
Akrotiri Wing, Cyprus: 9 and 35 Squadrons, 1969 to 1975
Coningsby Wing, Lincolnshire: 9, 12 and 35 Squadrons, 1962 to 1964
Cottesmore Wing, Rutland: 9, 12 and 35 Squadrons, 1964 to 1969
Finningley Wing, Yorkshire: 101 Squadron and 230 OCU, 1957 to 1969
Scampton Wing, Lincolnshire: 27, 35, 83, 617 Squadrons and 230 OCU, 1961 to 1982
Waddington Wing, Lincolnshire: 9, 44, 50, 83, 101 Squadrons and 230 OCU, 1960 to 1984

OTHER UNITS

Aeroplane & Armament Experimental Establishment, Boscombe Down, Wiltshire; Blind Landing Experimental Unit, Thurleigh, Bedfordshire; Bomber Command Development Unit, Finningley, Yorkshire; 4 Joint Services Trials Unit, Woomera, Australia; Royal Aircraft Establishment, Farnborough, Hampshire, and Thurleigh, Bedfordshire; Royal Radar Establishment, Pershore, Worcestershire; and - of course - the Vulcan Display Flight, Waddington, Lincolnshire, which flew XL426 and then XH558.

617 SQUADRON

Badge:	On a roundel, a wall in fesse, fracted by three flashes of lightning in pile and issuant from the breach of water proper. (Lightning bolts hitting a dam that has been breached.)
Motto:	Après moi, le deluge – After me, the flood
Previously flew:	English Electric Canberra B.6s to 1955
May 1, 1958	Re-formed at Scampton, Lincs, on Vulcan B.1s
Sep 1961	First Vulcan B.2s arrive
Dec 31, 1981	Disbanded
Post-Vulcan:	Re-formed on Panavia Tornado GR.1s 1983; disbanded in 2014 and - patiently - awaiting the introduction of the Lockheed Martin F-35B Joint Strike Fighter

B.2 on static display at an RAF Battle of Britain 'At Home' in September 1978 wearing the diamond badge of 617 Squadron, showing the unit's three lightning bolts plus a shattered dam and cascading water. KEC

XL392

THAT'S MY VULCAN!

The seventh Vulcan B.2, XH539, first flew at Woodford in May 1961. It joined the trials fleet of the Aeroplane & Armament Experimental Establishment at Boscombe Down, Wiltshire, in December 1967 and served the unit until it was retired in 1972. For around 20 days in August 1968 it carried the initials of Flt Lt Tim Mason - 'TM' - in giant letters on the fin, before this unauthorised decoration was removed. Alongside the lettering was the badge of Edwards Air Force Base, which was applied during a visit to the California test facility. Tim served as a test pilot at Boscombe Down from 1966 to 1976 and went on to become a well-known aviation historian and author.

Issued to 230 Operational Conversion Unit at Finningley in June 1962, XL387 carrying the white rose of Yorkshire. KEC

V-force Last of the

Charting whole extant Vulcans, Victors and Valiants

Right
Vulcan XH558 salutes the Vulcan Restoration Trust's taxiable XL426 at Southend Airport during the 'V-force Tour' of June 28, 2015. PHIL WHALLEY-AVPICS

V-BOMBERS - Intact surviving airframes

Serial	Variant	Status	Location and Notes	More
VULCANS				
XH558	B.2	Taxiable	Vulcan to the Sky Trust, Doncaster Sheffield Airport, Yorks. G-VLCN, *Spirit of Great Britain*	www.vulcantothesky.org
XJ823	B.2	Displayed	Solway Aviation Museum, Carlisle, Cumbria	www.solway-aviation-museum.co.uk
XJ824	B.2	Displayed	Imperial War Museum, Duxford, Cambs	www.iwm.org.uk
XL318	B.2	Displayed	RAF Museum, Hendon, London	www.rafmuseum.org
XL319	B.2	Displayed	North East Land, Sea and Air Museums, Usworth, Tyne and Wear	www.nelsam.org.uk
XL360	B.2	Displayed	Midland Air Museum, Coventry Airport, Warks. *City of Coventry*	www.midlandairmuseum.org.uk
XL361	B.2	Displayed	Canadian Forces, Goose Bay, Labrador, Canada	www.forces.gc.ca
XL426	B.2	Taxiable	Vulcan Restoration Trust, Southend, Essex. G-VJET. Maintained in taxiable condition	www.avrovulcan.com
XM573	B.2	Displayed	Strategic Air and Space Museum, Offutt, Nebraska, USA	www.strategicairandspace.com
XM575	B.2	Displayed	East Midlands Airport, Castle Donington, Leics. G-BLMC	www.eastmidlandsaeropark.org
XM594	B.2	Displayed	Newark Air Museum, Winthorpe, Notts	www.newarkairmuseum.org
XM597	B.2	Displayed	National Museum of Flight Scotland, East Fortune, Scotland	www.nms.ac.uk/flight
XM598	B.2	Displayed	RAF Museum, Cosford, Shropshire	www.rafmuseum.org
XM603	B.2	Displayed	Avro Heritage Centre, Woodford, Gtr Manchester	www.avroheritage.com
XM605	B.2	Displayed	Castle Air Museum, Atwater, California, USA	www.castleairmuseum.org
XM606	B.2	Displayed	Eighth Air Force Museum, Barksdale AFB, Louisiana, USA	www.8afmuseum.net
XM607	B.2	Displayed	RAF Waddington, Lincoln, Lincs	www.raf.mod.uk
XM612	B.2	Displayed	City of Norwich Aviation Museum, Horsham St Faith, Norfolk	www.cnam.co.uk
XM655	B.2	Taxiable	XM655 Maintenance and Preservation Society, Wellesbourne Mountford, Warks. G-VULC. Maintained in taxiable condition	www.xm655.com
VICTORS				
XH648	B.1A	Displayed	Imperial War Museum, Duxford, Cambs	www.iwm.org.uk
XH672	K.2	Displayed	RAF Museum, Cosford, Shropshire. *Maid Marian*	www.rafmuseum.org
XH673	K.2	Displayed	RAF Marham, Norfolk	www.raf.mod.uk
XM715	K.2	Taxiable	Cold War Jets, Bruntingthorpe, Leics. *Teasin' Tina*	www.bruntingthorpeaviation.com
XL231	K.2	Taxiable	Yorkshire Air Museum, Elvington, Yorkshire. *Lusty Lindy*	www.yorkshireairmuseum.org
VALIANT				
XD818	BK.1	Displayed	RAF Museum, Cosford, Shropshire	www.rafmuseum.org

Left
Wellesbourne Mountford is the home of the other taxiable Vulcan, XM655. Soon to join the ranks of the fast taxi 'club', XH558 paid an overhead visit on June 21, 2015.
MICHAEL MIKLOS

Below left
Valiant BK.1 XD818 – the only whole example extant – is displayed in the National Cold War Exhibition at the RAF Museum, Cosford.
KEY-STEVE FLETCHER

Below
Victor K.2 XH673 'guards' RAF Marham, the last operational base for the Handley Page V-bomber.
KEY-DUNCAN CUBITT

Above
RAF Waddington is 'guarded' by 'Black Buck' B.2 XM607.
KEN ELLIS

First & Last
Twice

Vulcan XH558 was the first B.2 to enter service with the RAF — 33 years later it started civilian life

Above right
Tony Blackman became a test pilot for Avro at Woodford in 1956 and delivered XH558 to the RAF in 1960. He was Chief Test Pilot at Woodford from 1970 to 1978.
BRITISH AEROSPACE-KEC

Tony Blackman strapped into Vulcan B.2 XH558 at its birthplace, Woodford, south of Manchester, on July 1, 1960, for what was an unusual sortie for an Avro test pilot. Alongside him, in the co-pilot's seat, was Wg Cdr C C 'Jock' Calder, the officer commanding 230 Operational Conversion Unit (OCU) at Waddington. Lincolnshire.

Ordinarily, once a Vulcan was declared off-test and ready for collection, an RAF crew would arrive at Woodford and deliver the delta to its unit. But XH558 was the first of the much-developed B.2 variant to be accepted for service. Although Wg Cdr Calder had many hours at the helm of the earlier B.1, he was not checked out on the new breed; hence Tony was the captain for the ferry fight.

Like many Vulcan aircrew, Jock had cut his teeth on the Vulcan's illustrious predecessor, the Lancaster. He had been a member of the famous 617 Squadron, the 'Dam Busters', and on March 14, 1945 had led the unit on a raid against the Bielefeld railway viaduct, near Paderborn, Germany. This impressive structure and impressive rail link was easy to locate at more than 1,000ft (304m) long, with 26

Above right
On July 1, 1960, Vulcan XH558, resplendent in white 'anti-flash' colours, touched down at Waddington to become the first B.2 to enter RAF service. AVRO-KEC

arches, but it was only 27ft wide. Previous attempts to bring it down had failed. His Lancaster was one of two carrying the 22,000lb (9,979kg) 'Grand Slam', or 'earthquake', bomb and the first to unleash the awesome weapon in anger. Jock's bomb fell about 80ft from the target, creating a 100ft deep crater that undermined and rocked the viaduct. Six arches collapsed.

Such was progress that, 15 years later, Jock Calder started to master the Vulcan B.2 that could carry 21,000lb of conventional weapons, but in 21 thousand-pounders, something well beyond the bomb bay of the 'Lanc'. The Vulcan could also fly at more than *twice* the speed and *four times* as far.

Not long after XH558 joined 230 OCU at Waddington, the unit moved to Finningley in Yorkshire. Forty-three years after XH558 departed that base, history repeated itself – on March 29, 2011 the Vulcan touched down on the same runway it used while training aircrew to again make Finningley its home. Both the airfield and the bomber had become civilians – as Robin Hood Doncaster Sheffield Airport and G-VLCN, respectively. As it transpired, this time the RAF's first Vulcan B.2 had become a *permanent* resident at its inaugural base.

"THE EXACT NATURE OF THE MRR ROLE HAS NEVER BEEN FULLY REVEALED. SOME OF THE DUTIES INVOLVED PATROLS – SOMETIMES AT CLOSE QUARTERS – AROUND NORTH SEA OIL RIGS. RUMOURS RELATING TO THE TASKING RANGED FROM 'SNIFFING' FOR SOVIET SUBMARINES TO THE MUCH MORE BENIGN CHECKING AIR QUALITY."

XH558 TIMELINE

May 21, 1960	First test flight at Woodford, the 12th B.2 built. Off-test and ready for collection on the 30th.
Jul 1, 1960	Delivered to 230 Operational Conversion Unit (OCU), 'B' Flight, at Waddington and taken on charge by the unit on the 8th.
Jun 16, 1961	No.230 OCU moved from Waddington to Finningley.
Sep 1963	Fitted with an in-flight refuelling probe, *perhaps* the first so equipped with 230 OCU.
Feb 11, 1964	To Hawker Siddeley for modifications; work completed Jun 29, 1964 and returned to 230 OCU.
Dec 15, 1966	To Hawker Siddeley for refit; work completed Feb 23, 1967.
Feb 26, 1968	Transferred to the Waddington Wing, centralised servicing comprising 44, 50 and 101 Squadrons.
Jun 4, 1969	To Hawker Siddeley for refit/mods; work completed Oct 14, 1969.
Dec 2, 1969	Involved in an unspecified Category 3R accident; repaired on site.
Oct 31, 1972	On charge with 101 Squadron at Waddington.
Aug 17, 1973	Issued to Hawker Siddeley at Bitteswell for conversion to B.2(MRR) maritime radar reconnaissance configuration - one of five full conversions (the others being XH534, XH537 XH560 and XH563) plus three without the ability to carry underwing air-sampling pods (XJ780, XJ823 and XJ825).
Sep 17, 1974	Issued to 27 Squadron at Waddington.
Nov 6, 1975	Suffered bird strike on take-off from Scampton; successful return to base but damage to Nos 3 and 4 engines and surrounding area.
Oct 18, 1976	On temporary attachment to 230 OCU at Scampton. (The OCU moved from Finningley to the Lincolnshire base in Dec 1969.)
Nov 29, 1976	Returned to 27 Squadron at Waddington.
Mar 31, 1982	Transferred to the Waddington Wing, centralised servicing comprising 9, 44, 50 and 101 Squadrons. Retained air-sampling pods from its 27 Squadron days and placed on charge with 44 Squadron.
Jun 30, 1982	To British Aerospace, Woodford, for conversion to K.2 tanker. (Last of six converted, others were: XH560, XH561, XJ825, XL445 and XM571.) Jul 5, 1982
Oct 12, 1982	Work completed, issued to 50 Squadron at Waddington.
Oct 25, 1982	To Aeroplane & Armament Experimental Establishment, Boscombe Down. Trials completed by Nov 30 and returned to 50 Squadron.
Apr 1, 1984	Transferred to the charge of Waddington Station Flight.
Sep 17, 1984	Delivered to Marham for use as a fire fighting airframe. When it was realised XH558 had more available flying hours, it was returned to Waddington and XH560 took its place at Marham on Nov 29, 1984.
Nov 14, 1984	Taken on charge with the Vulcan Display Flight (VDF), Waddington. Over the winter of 1984/1985 it was 'de-converted' to B.2 status and was then held in reserve.
Jun 14, 1986	Replaced XL426 as current VDF aircraft.
Sep 20, 1992	Final display sortie, at Cranfield; returned to Waddington following day.
Feb 1993	Ministry of Defence issued documentation inviting purchase of XH558 by tender.
Mar 23, 1993	Delivered to Bruntingthorpe and struck off RAF charge.

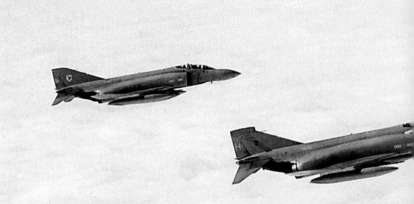

FIRST IN SERVICE

Avro Type 698 Vulcan B.2 XH558 was ordered under Ministry of Defence contract number 6/Acft/11301/Cb.6(a), placed on September 30, 1954, for 17 examples. Partially 'plumbed' for the abortive Douglas GAM-87A Skybolt long-range nuclear stand-off weapon with mountings underwing, XH558 was to later make use of these seemingly useless items

Built at Woodford, it took to the air for the first time on May 21. When Tony Blackman and Jock Calder delivered to XH558 to Waddington on July 1 it became the first Mk.2 to enter RAF service. It was issued to 'B' Flight of 230 OCU - 'A' Flight trained B.1 crews.

The OCU's initial task was to train personnel for 83 Squadron, the first operational B.2 unit, which took on its first aircraft at Scampton, Lincolnshire, in December 1960. Finningley became the new home for 230 OCU on June 18, 1961 and XH558 remained on charge for the next eight years until, in February 1968, it returned to 'Wadders'. (See the panel for full details of XH558's service career.)

There XH558 became part of the Waddington Wing under the centralised servicing scheme. At this time the wing comprised 44, 50 and 101 Squadrons, but individual squadron allocations came into vogue again and XH558 was wearing 101 Squadron insignia in late 1972.

MARITIME 'SPOOK'

In August 1973, XH558 left Waddington for Bitteswell, Leicestershire, where Hawker Siddeley Aviation carried out a conversion to B.2(MRR) maritime radar reconnaissance standard. Work included fitment of the forward and aft facing passive electronic countermeasures antennae atop the fin, removal of the terrain following radar 'thimble' installation and fitting an array of electronic installations in the bomb-bay and elsewhere. Five of the eight MRRs could have air-sampling pods fitted to the long-redundant Skybolt fixtures under the wing: XH558 was one of these.

On completion, XH558 was delivered to 27 Squadron at Scampton in September 1974. The unit was partially taking up the role previously carried out by the Handley Page Victor SR.2s of Wyton-based 543 Squadron, which had disbanded the previous May. The exact nature of the MRR role has never been fully revealed. Some of the duties involved patrols – sometimes at close quarters – around North Sea oil rigs. Rumours relating to the tasking ranged from

"FOLLOWING A REQUEST FROM THE MINISTRY OF DEFENCE FOR EXTRA TANKER CAPACITY, BRITISH AEROSPACE AT WOODFORD RECEIVED AN IMMEDIATE ORDER FOR SIX VULCAN TANKER CONVERSIONS ON APRIL 30, 1982... AT WADDINGTON, 50 SQUADRON RECEIVED ITS FIRST K.2, XH561, ON JUNE 23 – JUST 51 DAYS AFTER THE GO-AHEAD!"

'sniffing' for Soviet submarines to the much more benign checking air quality.

As a B.2(MRR), XH558 remained with 27 Squadron until March 1982 when it returned to the Waddington Wing. Initially it kept the underwing air-sampling pods.

STOP-GAP TANKERS
The Vulcan's final operational role was as a tanker to help the already hard-pressed Victor K.2 fleet – these crescent-winged beauties had worked wonders during the Falklands crisis. Always considered to be a stop-gap measure, the distinctly utilitarian housing beneath the K.2's tail can be forgiven – it was certainly the worst-ever blemish to an exceptionally clean design.

Following a request from the Ministry of Defence for extra tanker capacity, British Aerospace at Woodford received an immediate order for six Vulcan tanker conversions on April 30, 1982. The first test flew on June 18 and the single-point tanker was released for service five days later. At Waddington, 50 Squadron received its first K.2, XH561, on June 23 – just 51 days after the go-ahead! The last of the six to be converted, XH558 was delivered back to Waddington in October 1982, this time joining 50 Squadron.

Ignoring the speed of the conversion, the K.2 was no mean feat of engineering. The hose drum unit was mounted in what had been the electronic countermeasures bay in the tail, with a shed-like fairing of wood and metal below it containing the drogue and the 'traffic light' signals array for the receiving aircraft. The copious Vulcan bomb-bay carried three plumbed-in cylindrical tanks of similar design to the extra-range modifications the bomber could always opt for.

On December 17, 1982, Strike Command staged a special photo-session at Waddington in which B.2s XL391, XM597, XM607 and XM612 flew a farewell salute to the bomber variant of the mighty delta. Five days later, 44 Squadron, the unit that had 'parented' the Falklands 'Black Buck' deployment, disbanded. Time was running out for the Vulcan.

'Strike' staged *another* 'farewell' event at the Lincolnshire base on March 14, 1984 to mark the passing of the K.2-equipped 50 Squadron. With this event, the delta evolved from operational to retiree. Other than currency flights and deliveries to museums, it looked as though there would be no more Vulcans to thrill the crowds. Could nothing be done?

SHOWTIME!
The day after 50 Squadron laid down its colours and disbanded, on April 1, 1984, the RAF gained a new unit, the Vulcan Display Flight (VDF). Prior to this Vulcans had been flown at airshows via the all-volunteer Vulcan Display Team, essentially an element of 55 Squadron, the unit flying Victor K.2s tankers out of Marham, Norfolk. Acting as a 'lodger' within the Waddington Station Flight, VDF was issued with B.2 XL426 and for the 1984 to 1987 seasons, it performed at a select number of airshows.

With the disbandment of 50 Squadron, XH558 was transferred to the Waddington Station Flight, pending its disposal. On September 17, 1984, the delta was flown to Marham, Norfolk; where it had been allocated for fire-rescue training. When it was realised it had plenty of flying hours available, this fate was rescinded and in November it was selected for the VDF and returned to Waddington.

The Vulcan underwent what was called a Service Embodied Modification during the winter of 1984/1985 and re-flew in April

November 1985, XH558 was ready for the forthcoming display season and replaced XL426, which was put up for disposal. A new life as a heritage display aircraft kicked off in May 1986 at Bournemouth, the first of many popular displays.

With XH558 as the sole remaining operational example, consumable spares were sought from all over the RAF and brought to Waddington. Replacements for many items in the inventory would simply not be possible once stocks were used up. The future of XH558 depended not just on care and attention to

had to dawn, and it was declared that 1992 would be XH558's – and therefore the type's – last 'season'.

Packed into a Lyneham Tactical Wing Lockheed Hercules C.1, still and video cameramen clicked away furiously on September 7, 1992 as XH558 made a sortie on behalf of the media for a last-ever air-to-air session. Ten days later the Vulcan taxied out at Waddington to embark on its last public appearances, with a flight down to the Channel Islands for Jersey and Guernsey's Battle of Britain celebrations, then a long positioning run to Leuchars in Scotland, in

Below
In XH558's final flying season with the RAF, 1992, campaigning to keep the delta in the air was intense.

Below right
The VDT mascot clocked up a serious amount of flying time in the bomb aimer's position.
BOTH KEY-DUNCAN CUBITT

Above, right to left
Display flight badges: The Vulcan Association's 'RAF Display Flight' patch; Panther's head on the VDT patch; and a stylised 'V' behind a Vulcan saluting Lincoln Cathedral painted on XH558's access door.
KEY-DUNCAN CUBITT

1985 in an external configuration almost exactly the same as when it had been an operational V-bomber.

Between September and November 1985, XH558 was resprayed at Kinloss in Scotland into gloss camouflage with the Lincoln coat of arms on the tail fin (signifying the freedom of the City of Lincoln), a 'Union Jack' and, on either side of the fuselage forward of the intakes, the panther's head emblem of 1 Group, Strike Command. These markings were chosen because they were carried by all Vulcans taking part in the USAF's Strategic Air Command 'Giant Voice' bombing and navigation competitions and were, therefore, representative of all the units during the 1970s.

Returned to Waddington in

all maintenance schedules, but to precise calculations of consumption of major items, sparing use of flying hours and a constant search for hitherto 'lost' parts. Something as lowly as the tyre stocks could ground the mighty delta forever.

ALL GOOD THINGS...

A Vulcan performing under RAF aegis at airshows could only last for so long. Its public appeal was fantastic – it continued to be the show-stopper. It may sound like heresy to say so, but it seemed to rival the 'Red Arrows' for popularity.

Few would have thought that the Ministry of Defence and the RAF would allow such a complex, costly and asset-consuming beast to fly on for another nine years. Reality

readiness for the station's Battle of Britain 'At Home' show. From there it went to its former home at Finningley for the second 'At Home' of the day, and an overnight stop.

Cranfield's 'Dreamflight' show was destined to be XH558's last-ever RAF public display. At the Bedfordshire airfield the Vulcan was flanked by the Hawks of the 'Red Arrows' aerobatic team.

WHAT NEXT?

The Vulcan's following, especially in its last couple of years, was immense. After the announcement that the VDF was to stop flying at the end of the 1992 season and XH558 was to be sold off by tender, the public response sent shock waves all around the Ministry of

"ON THE MORNING OF SEPTEMBER 21, 1992 A HUGE CROWD ASSEMBLED ALONG THE A15 ROAD BORDERING THE EASTERN SIDE OF WADDINGTON. THE PUBLIC WERE GOING TO PAY HOMAGE ONE LAST TIME. "

Defence. Here was an aircraft that united a staggering number of taxpayers – and voters.

In the very year that XH558 faced being pensioned off, the largest supporter organisation of its kind anywhere at the time – the Vulcan Association – collapsed, just when a national campaign needed such a co-ordinating body.

Into the gap came a series of determined people who worked hard through the summer of 1992, encouraging all and sundry to sign petitions to Downing Street, the Ministry of Defence, Strike Command and to lobby MPs. It was to no avail – the decision stood.

On the morning of September 21, a huge crowd assembled along the A15 road bordering the eastern side of Waddington. The public were going to pay homage one last time.

At 10am, XH558 departed Cranfield and made a straight-in, no-frills, approach to Waddington at 25 minutes past the hour. Everyone knew that it was just possible that the Vulcan had made its, the RAF's and the type's, last-ever flight.

On January 27, 1993 the MoD confirmed that XH558 was to be put up for sale. The documents inviting bids by tender were issued in the week beginning February 1. Everything came down to just who – if anybody – was planning to acquire the Vulcan. Thankfully, moves were afoot to give XH558 a chance at a whole stack of new 'firsts'...

For more on XH558's early days with the RAF turn to page 44.

The pace of development in the 1940s and 1950s was such that only 11 years separated the first flights of the Lancaster and the Vulcan. XH558 and the Battle of Britain Memorial Flight Lancaster PA474 saluting Lincoln Cathedral, August 2014. *JOHN DIBBS © 2015*

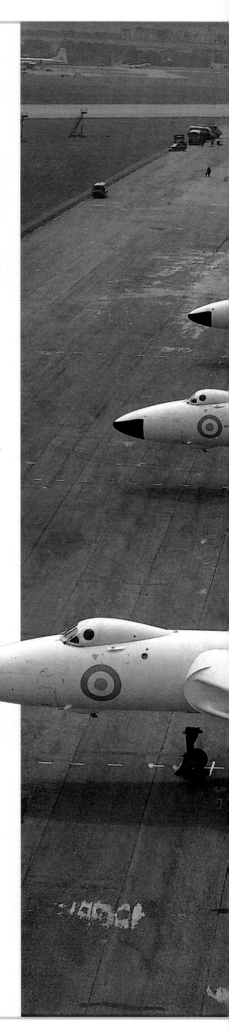

Show of Force

With the much improved Vulcan B.2 coming on strength, the RAF was keen to show off its new bomber

Vulcan B.2 XH558 was the first of the variant to enter service with the RAF, joining 230 Operational Conversion Unit (OCU) at Waddington in July 1960. The delta's first task was to prepare aircrew destined for the first frontline unit, 83 Squadron.

Based at Waddington, 83 flew B.1s from July 1957, moving to Scampton in October 1960, ready to receive its first B.2s. Less than two months old, B.2 XH563 was taken on charge on December 28.

The next Vulcan B.2 squadron was 27, which re-formed at Scampton – alongside the pioneering 83 – on April 1, 1961. Its first B.2 was XJ823, which arrived at the Lincolnshire base on April 21, just 22 days after its inaugural test flight off the production line at Woodford, near Manchester.

Three weeks was an impressive time to 'shake down' such a complex aircraft from first flight and declare it ready for collection by the RAF. This was a fine testament to the quality of work by the Avro workforce and the efficiency of the test pilots at Woodford who regularly combined to achieve such a brisk pace. (See XL318, below.)

PRESS LINE-UP

Thumbing through the Key Publishing archives, a series of images marked 'Exercise Mayflight, May 1961' caught the eye of *FlyPast* editor Nigel Price. Images of an impressive line-up of nine all-white Vulcan B.2s brought the magnifying glass into action and there, in the middle of the gathering, was none

other than XH558!

'Mayflight' was a regular exercise, deploying the Vulcan force to other airfields, often ones that were not 'bread and butter' venues for Bomber Command crews. Normally 'simple' cross-countries, they were designed to familiarise aircrew with airspace and the surrounding area. If the 'Cold War' were to turn 'hot', then the very survival of the V-force was dependent on a swift and efficient scattering away from base.

In May 1961 members of the press were invited to visit Scampton to marvel at nine Vulcans wingtip to wingtip and then watch as the deltas blasted off to head west. The images in the archive enabled the serial numbers of all the participating Vulcans to be read and it *seems* that 230 OCU, from the other side of Lincoln at Waddington, had been roped in to help make the numbers up!

At the head of the nine Vulcans, B.2 XJ782 proudly wore the Royal Blue and Air Force Blue triangular pennant with two red stripes to denote it was 'owned' by a wing commander; between that and the nose roundel was the badge of 83 Squadron. Delivered in the middle of the previous January, XJ782 was parked alongside another three of 83's B.2s. (See the panel for details.)

In the middle was an example from the other Scampton resident unit, 27 Squadron – XJ823. Furthest from the lenses of the gathering photographers were four machines from 230 OCU, including the already historic (as the first B.2 delivered to an RAF

"IMAGES OF AN IMPRESSIVE LINE-UP OF NINE ALL-WHITE VULCAN B.2S BROUGHT THE MAGNIFYING GLASS INTO ACTION AND THERE, IN THE MIDDLE OF THE GATHERING, WAS NONE OTHER THAN XH558!"

SCAMPTON VULCAN LINE-UP | MAY 1961

Serial	First unit and base	Taken on Charge	Disposal or current whereabouts
XJ782	83 Sqn, Scampton	Mar 2, 1961	Scrapped 1988
XJ783	83 Sqn, Scampton	Mar 13, 1961	Scrapped 1982
XH554	83 Sqn, Scampton	Apr 10, 1961	RAF Fire Fighting School, Catterick, 1981
XH563	83 Sqn, Scampton	Dec 28, 1960	Scrapped 1986; cockpit extant
XJ823	27 Sqn, Scampton	Apr 21, 1961	Preserved at Carlisle
XH558	230 OCU, Waddington	Jul 1, 1960	Vulcan to the Sky, Finningley
XH562	230 OCU, Waddington	Dec 9, 1960	RAF Fire Fighting School, Catterick, 1982
XH561	230 OCU, Waddington	Nov 11, 1960	RAF Fire Fighting School, Catterick, 1984
XH559	230 OCU, Waddington	Aug 24, 1960	Scrapped 1982

unit, and eventually a national icon) XH558. No matter what the reason was for the inclusion of deltas from the OCU in the press presentation, nine Vulcans raring to go was an awesome sight and it was not wasted on Bomber Command's guests.

LEGITIMATE LEADER

"I'm the only Bastard in the RAF or, at least, the only one who'll admit it!" Many RAF personnel have quoted this, or similar wording, as the catchphrase of a man who was clearly well respected and admired: Laurence George Aggitt Bastard. On September 1, 1961 Wg Cdr George Bastard lifted Vulcan B.2 XL318 off from Woodford to ferry it to Scampton.

The arrival of XL318 at the

> "'I'M THE ONLY BASTARD IN THE RAF OR, AT LEAST, THE ONLY ONE WHO'LL ADMIT IT!' MANY RAF PERSONNEL HAVE QUOTED THIS AS THE CATCHPHRASE OF A MAN WHO WAS CLEARLY WELL RESPECTED AND ADMIRED."

base was eagerly awaited by 617 Squadron – the 'Dam Busters'. George was proud to be the famous unit's commanding officer, a post he held from 1960 to 1962. He presided over the transition from the Vulcan B.1 to the B.2 – and helped to prepare the way to operational readiness with the 'Blue Steel' stand-off missile, which was achieved in February 1963.

Flown for the first time 22 days before George picked it up from Woodford, XL318 was 617's first of the new variant, the squadron having flown B.1s since May 1958. An intense period of exercises and deployments was established as more B.2s were accepted on strength at Scampton and, in the autumn of 1961, the 'Dam Busters' showed off its B.2s with a mock 'scramble'.

BOMBER BOY

George Bastard was a 'Bomber Boy' through and through. After training he moved to the Whitley-equipped 10 Operational Training Unit at Stanton Harcourt, near Oxford, finishing off on the ubiquitous Wellington. Then he was bound for Yorkshire and 1652 Heavy Conversion Unit at Marston Moor where he converted to Halifaxes.

As a flying officer, he completed 22 'ops' with 10 Squadron from January 1945, piloting Halifax IIIs from Melbourne, southeast of York. He converted to Canberras in the mid-1950s and in January 1957 became Sqn Ldr Bastard AFC.

At 230 OCU at Waddington, George learned to master the mighty Avro delta before taking command of 617 Squadron. After his stint with the 'Dam Busters', he enjoyed

Right
The 'press end' of the May 1961 line-up at Scampton, framed by the 83 Squadron CO's XJ782.

Below
All kitted up, a crew at full tilt towards their Vulcan.
ALL KEY COLLECTION

an exchange posting with Strategic Air Command in the USA, where he captained the eight-engined Boeing B-52 Stratofortress.

From 1969 to 1971 he was the officer commanding at Cottesmore, which was home to the electronic countermeasures Canberra-equipped 98 Squadron and 115 Squadron with Varsity T.1s.

MUSEUM PIECE

Vulcan B.2 XL318 remained remarkably loyal to 617 Squadron. During much of 1962 the bomber carried 'Blue Steel' training rounds to get aircrew used to the large missile semi-recessed in the bomb bay. On May 6, 1963 the V-bomber was part of another Exercise 'Mayflight', in this case a deployment to the massive US base at Burtonwood near Warrington.

In May 1972, XL318 departed Scampton bound for 230 OCU at Finningley before returning to the 'Dam Busters' in March 1974. In June 1975 it made the short hop from Scampton to Waddington, joining the pooled fleet of 9, 44, 50 and 101 Squadrons. This lasted just two months before it rejoined the OCU.

The 'pull' of 617 was strong and XL318 returned to the fold at Scampton on the first day of July 1981. This was a necessarily short-term 'posting' as the unit was destined to disband on the last day of the year before it re-emerged in January 1983 with Tornado GR.1s at Marham. Wg Cdr John Herbertson, 617's 'boss', took XL318 for its last flight on

December 11. The first B.2 on charge with the 'Dam Busters', XL318 also had the honour of carrying out the last Vulcan sortie with the unit.

With such a pedigree, it was not surprising that XL318 had been earmarked for a new role: it was destined for the Bomber Command Hall at the RAF Museum, Hendon. During January and February 1982 the challenging task of dismantling the Vulcan and taking it south by road to the yet-to-be-completed building at Hendon was conducted.

Carefully positioned inside as construction work continued around it, XL318 was back in one piece by June 1982 ready for the official opening of the emotive tribute to the men and machines of Bomber Command. ◦

"WITH SUCH A PEDIGREE, IT WAS NOT SURPRISING THAT XL318 HAD BEEN EARMARKED FOR A NEW ROLE: IT WAS DESTINED FOR THE BOMBER COMMAND HALL AT THE RAF MUSEUM, HENDON."

Vulcan to the Sky

How do you take a redundant V-bomber and turn it into a civilian-operated warbird? Ken Ellis explains how thousands of supporters, individual and corporate, combined to achieve the Vulcan's return to flight

"*Marshall 15* is ready for departure," was the call from the cockpit at Bruntingthorpe, Leicestershire, 12:26 local time on Thursday, October 18, 2007. It had dawned cold, misty, but with high pressure dominant. It looked to be a settled, gorgeous autumnal day. All the better for the making of aviation history!

Vulcan B.2 XH558, civil registration G-VLCN, was about to take to the air, no longer as an RAF V-bomber, but as the most powerful warbird ever flown.

A large number of guests, supporters, representatives of the aviation industry and other organisations had been invited. Also flocking into the Leicestershire airfield were the media ready to beam the news all over the planet. So, no pressure then...

Excited spectators made their way to Bruntingthorpe's 9,800ft (3,000m) runway while XH558 was towed to its dispersal. Taking the delta back into the sky were Sqn Ldr David Thomas, chief pilot; Sqn Ldr Al McDicken, pilot and Barry Masefield, air electronics officer (AEO).

At the threshold of Runway 24, on went the power. Climbing out with all the vigour that the delta was renowned for, off she flew towards the east for basic handling up to 250 knots.

After a practice approach that was almost drowned out by the clicking of cameras and thunderous applause, the Vulcan turned downwind and made a perfect touchdown at 12:58. As the crew disembarked, the greeting from the crowd was euphoric.

BUYING A V-BOMBER

The year 1993 was not a good one for fans of real jets. Six days before the Ministry of Defence (MoD) announced the sale by tender of recently retired Vulcan XH558, the English Electric Lightning had made its last sortie under RAF control: F.6 XS904 was delivered to Bruntingthorpe to join the Lightning Preservation Group. The last of the faithful Handley Page Victor K.2 tanker fleet made its final flight that November when XH672 touched down at Shawbury, Shropshire, on the 30th prior to moving by road to the RAF Museum at nearby Cosford.

Normally, the MoD was not allowed to influence the tender process; but it was clear that national regard for XH558 needed to be considered. Those hoping to purchase the bomber had to provide details of their intentions and how these would be carried out. The unspoken ground rules were fairly straightforward: the RAF's last Vulcan was not going to be cut up or mutilated and it was not for export. However, the highly competitive and cost-conscious Conservative Government also wanted it to go to the highest bidder.

Among those bidding was David Walton. The holder of a private pilots licence since 1981, he had long been fascinated with aviation and military jets in particular. He was also a successful businessman and he owned an airfield. He and his family ran Bruntingthorpe and a variety of enterprises from it. The family also wanted to open a museum, which gelled as the Cold War Jets Collection in 1999.

Far left
Dr Robert Pleming discussing the maiden flight with Sqn Ldr Al McDicken, surrounded by camera crews.

Below
Moment of history: XH558 takes to the air at Bruntingthorpe on October 18, 2007.
ALL KEY-DUNCAN CUBITT UNLESS NOTED

"AT THE THRESHOLD OF RUNWAY 24, ON WENT THE POWER. CLIMBING OUT WITH ALL THE VIGOUR THAT THE DELTA WAS RENOWNED FOR, OFF SHE FLEW TOWARDS THE EAST..."

FIRST FLIGHT COMMENTS

After XH558's first flight as a civilian, members of the team expressed their thoughts. From the left:

Sqn Ldr Al McDicken (pilot): "It's rather dull to say this, but there were no problems at all. There was an air of intense concentration inside the cockpit and we just got on with it; she behaved perfectly."

Sqn Ldr David Thomas (chief pilot): "She performed just like she did with the Vulcan Display Flight. The initial rotation was pretty impressive, on climb-out we noted that we were making 4,000ft per minute!"

Sqn Ldr Barry Masefield (AEO): Many of the press couldn't get their head around Barry's role - monitoring all the systems - so he helped them out: "My station is best described as a broom cupboard with a Hoover on and the light out... I fly facing backwards, so while I know where I've been, I've no idea where I'm being taken!"

Cpl Kevin 'Taff' Stone (crew chief): "This morning we towed her out and I was asked, 'Can we close the [hangar] doors?' I said, 'Shut them, she's not going back until she's flown!' "

Dr Robert Pleming (VTS CEO): "We now need to change gear from restoration to keeping her flying... this will be a real challenge. ...The Vulcan's story enters a new chapter, providing inspiration and education. We must keep this icon in the air to allow it to fulfil this vital mission."

Andrew Edmondson (engineering manager): "The OEMs and the engineers have been vital to this incredible project. ...What has been achieved is best described as engineering archaeology."

The Waltons carefully put together their proposal. Just how much they offered for XH558 has never been confirmed, but £25,000 was probably near to the target. The spending didn't stop there. They very wisely went for the huge spares holding also available, which included Bristol Siddeley Olympus 202 turbojets – still in their crates and fully documented. All of this came to 40-odd lorryloads. This 'add-on' purchase showed phenomenal foresight.

The MoD churned its way through the 43 bids and sent back 11 as ineligible. Of those returned, two were from scrap merchants and it is likely at some would have been from overseas.

Looking back, the C Walton (Aviation Division) tender really did 'tick all the boxes'. The company had a runway, which would make delivery easy. The plan was to keep XH558 in the UK, in one piece, indoors, at least in taxiable condition, to show it off to the public on suitable occasions and eventually open a museum. And the bid included the spares to sustain 'live' operation. Job done!

A NEW HOME

Summoned to Waddington on March 18, 1993, the Walton family found the press, radio and television crews gathering, ready for an announcement. Air Cdre David Hurrell, Senior Staff Officer of 38 Group, introduced David to the media as the highest bidder. Asked if he was going to keep XH558 flying, David said: "In the short term, the likelihood of the aircraft taking to the skies again is somewhat remote, but who knows what the long-term future may hold?"

Captained by Sqn Ldr Paul Millikin with Sqn Ldr David Thomas as co-pilot, Vulcan B.2 XH558 taxied out at Waddington ready for the type's final RAF sortie on March 23, 1993. A huge crowd thronged to pay their respects as it departed what was about to become a former V-bomber base.

After take-off, the delta did a low flypast, with the bomb doors open to reveal the FAREWELL lettering from its last months as a display aircraft the previous year. Woodford, Coningsby, Cottesmore, Marham, Scampton and Lincoln Cathedral were all overflown, before course was set for Leicestershire.

> "WOODFORD, CONINGSBY, COTTESMORE, MARHAM, SCAMPTON AND LINCOLN CATHEDRAL WERE ALL OVERFLOWN, BEFORE COURSE WAS SET FOR LEICESTERSHIRE."

Above
Inside Bruntingthorpe's 'Butler' hangar in 1996.

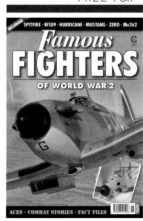
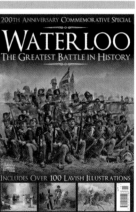

An enormous welcome awaited XH558 at its new home. As the engines shut down, amid a public and emotional ceremony, David accepted the documentation.

During the summer of 1993, XH558 was moved inside the huge former USAF 'Butler' hangar. To emphasise the family's commitment, Terry Smith, a former Hawker Siddeley employee at nearby Bitteswell where Vulcan modification and overhaul work had been carried out, started full-time at Bruntingthorpe in August. In effect, he was running a 'care and maintenance' programme.

The bulk of Terry's job was tackling the enormous spares cache that David had acquired. Truck after truck brought in around 600 tonnes, mostly from the cavernous RAF store at Stafford, comprising an estimated 250,000 pieces of crucial components. The non-military status of XH558 was emphasised on February 6, 1995 when it was civilian registered as G-VLCN.

> "THE RESTORATION OF THE AIRFRAME, ITS POWERPLANTS AND SYSTEMS WAS A HUGE UNDERTAKING, REQUIRING THE CO-OPERATION AND INPUT FROM MANY QUARTERS OF THE AEROSPACE SECTOR."

GETTING SERIOUS

Vulcan 'guru' Colin Mears launched the XH558 Supporters' Club in April 1997. A more loosely framed 'Friends of 558' had been established in late 1992, but under Colin's guidance a formal real back-up structure, pressure-group and fund-raising body had been founded. The existence of this organisation was to prove vital to the continued success of the scheme.

Taking the long-term view, David turned to Dr Robert Pleming to assess what was possible. Long since fascinated by the Cold War era and the Vulcan in particular,

Robert brought skills to the table that proved crucial. At that time was taking a 'leave of absence' from global information technology specialist Cisco Systems.

Negotiations started with British Aerospace (BAe - the design authority, from November 1999 renamed BAE Systems) and the Civil Aviation Authority (CAA - the regulatory body) to discuss what would be needed to fly a Vulcan as a civilian. An experienced project manager, Robert's style was one of preparation, patience and persistence. When met with a 'No' to a proposal, he would reformulate

the approach and find out what circumstances would be necessary to bring about a 'Yes'.

Where others would see a brick wall ahead, Robert would want to examine other routes through, over or around.

In mid-1999 it was announced that contacts with BAe and the CAA had borne fruit with an agreement in principle that XH558 could be brought back to airworthy status. From this the Vulcan Operating Company (VOC) was formed, with the middle word being the all-important one.

SOFT START

From the formation of VOC, work moved forward in two interdependent, but separate regimes. The restoration of the airframe, its powerplants and systems was a huge undertaking, requiring the co-operation and input from many quarters of the aerospace sector.

When the Vulcan was built in 1960 the abbreviation OEMs – Original Equipment Manufacturers - did not exist but 40 years later, they were crucial to the project. Many of these no longer traded

under their original names from the time when they were Avro sub-contractors, but after buyouts, mergers and takeovers, they were still part of some present-day organisation.

Alongside the engineering task was fund-raising and sponsorship. The XH558 Supporters' Club certainly had a big part to play in this, but the main aim was to find major financial backers. It was estimated that about £3 million was required for a first flight in 2001. While this looked a daunting sum to aircraft restorers, it was pointed out that this was

Above left
Work on the wing panels, May 2007. Amid all the tools and boxes, the air brakes are deployed.

Above
Crew chief 'Taff' Stone overseeing a wiring check in the bomb bay.
BOTH KEY-STEVE FLETCHER

Below
Vulcan XH558 out of the 'Butler' hangar in August 2006.

"LONG-TERM STALWARTS OF XH558 IN MANY WAYS, 'FLYPAST' READERS WERE CONTRIBUTING DIRECTLY AND VIA MAGAZINE INITIATIVES. NIGEL PRICE PRESENTED A CHEQUE FOR £2,000 IN FEBRUARY 2004..."

Below
Rolling out XH558 on October 18, 2007.

peanuts in the world of Formula 1 motor racing.

To provide a sure basis from which to move forward, teams from Cambridge-based major MOD contractor Marshall Aerospace arrived at Bruntingthorpe from November 15, 1999. Over a period of eight weeks they carried out a major inspection, coupled with structural integrity, engine and system functionality tests. Essentially, this was a 'health check' for XH558 and the delta was found to generally be up for the task ahead.

From this assessment, the way was clear to establish a workshop and stores to meet the CAA's A8-20 requirements to enable the aircraft to be eventually granted a 'Complex' category Permit to Fly. Joining the team in late 1999, initially as crew chief, was Trevor Bailey who had previously been a prime mover in bringing the Vulcan Restoration Trust's XL426 back to taxying status at Southend.

Robert came on board full-time from April 2000, leaving his high-profile post with Cisco to oversee the programme. His first priority was making an

application to the Heritage Lottery Fund (HLF). Around the same time Andrew Edmondson joined VOC as engineering manager.

Prior to the Vulcan, aircraft candidates for lottery monies to help towards a restoration to flying condition had been unsuccessful. So VOC pitched the educational and inspirational qualities of the project.

By early 2001 the term 'Vulcan to the Sky' (VTS) had been devised to provide a simple yet graphic 'vision' of the intention. Joining the team as patron was the former 'boss' of 1 Group Strike Command, 1980-1981, Sir Michael Knight, chairman of Cobham Aviation Services and president of the Air League.

Engineers on site by 2001 totalled nine full-time staff and the work moved into what was called the 'Soft Start' phase. By June, XH558 was effectively stripped bare, ready to give technicians fast access to all the 'deep' areas of the airframe.

Fund-raising was going well, but the the millions needed were not flowing in. Without a major sponsor, or a successful HLF bid, VOC was 'betting the farm'.

VALUE FOR MONEY?

By January 2003 more than 100 aerospace companies, including all

of the OEMs that had created the systems for the Vulcan had signed up. If even one of these critical sub-contractors had not co-operated, it could have had major – if not terminal – implications for VTS.

To illustrate the complexity of the Vulcan and the vital role of the OEMs, Avro dealt with 13 companies to create just one of the AEO's panels. By mid-2002 4,212 parts and sub-assemblies – weighing in at more than six tonnes – had been dispatched for inspection and servicing.

One of the OEMs, and obviously a major contributor, was Rolls-Royce. During early 2003 the company started what were called 'confidence checks' on the Olympus 202s to assess them, and a test-rig was devised on-site to help in this process. Throughout, Rolls-Royce helped in a great many ways.

Marshall Aerospace remained committed to the scheme and it became the project's engineering authority. In September 2001, Marshall applied to the CAA for formal approval to proceed to the next stage. At this point, VTS needed to prove it could afford Marshall's services and a contract had to be signed between them.

Then came a massive blow: on

November 15 it was announced that HLF had turned down the VTS grant application. Among the reasons given was that the fund did not support flying aircraft, yet it was happy with floating ships, motoring cars and chuffing locomotives. Additionally, the lottery felt that the project's timespan was too short and that it "did not represent value for money".

In the spring of 2003 HLF suggested that VTS should re-apply. Frantic consultation and much midnight-oil burning resulted in a 740-page plan including new initiatives: fine-tuning the education programme, establishing the Vulcan to the Sky Trust (VTST); purchasing XH558 from the Walton family and gifting it to the nation upon final retirement.

With the ink drying on this huge tome, VTST and the supporters club got into gear to raise £0.5 million by the end of 2003 so that the hoped-for funding required by HLF could be matched. Pledges of cash were sought that could be called in if the lottery gave approval. It was going to be a long and nail-biting year.

GREEN LIGHT

Christmas came early for everyone at Bruntingthorpe on December 11 when HLF announced a 'Stage One Pass', with £2,378,000 earmarked. Liz Forgam, the fund's chair, said: "In the normal way of things, we do not restore aircraft to flight but the HLF was really impressed with the imaginative way in which the [VTS] Trust's new proposal will let as many people as possible learn about this important part of their heritage."

By this stage, pledges from supporters – individual and corporate – had been arriving at the VTST office at an average of £10,000 per day and £1.3 million was held in the 'fighting' fund. In July 2004, the final details were ironed out and the grant was 'go'.

Long-term stalwarts of XH558 in many ways, *FlyPast* readers were contributing directly and via magazine initiatives. *FlyPast's* Nigel Price presented a cheque for £2,000 in February 2004 – the proceeds of the sale of a special 50th anniversary patch. Special editions of the Osprey book *Vulcan: Last of the V-Bombers* illustrated by *FlyPast* chief photographer Duncan Cubitt were handed over for sale by the supporters' club. Key Publishing further underlined its support with the indefinite loan its former travelling sales and publicity trailer for conversion into an exhibition unit for VTST.

With the establishment of the trust, the opportunity was undertaken to rename the XH558 Supporters' Club. From May 2 it became the Vulcan to the Sky Club and its fund-raising and support work remained vital to the project.

Above
*Some of the huge number
of well-wishers gathered
to watch an event they
had long anticipated and
all contributed towards.*

Below
*Coming over the
'numbers' at the end of
Bruntingthorpe's
Runway 24.*

RE-ASSEMBLY

After the approval of HLF, the next major milestone was the transfer of XH558 from C Walton (Aviation Division) to VTST, acting as custodian for the nation. The paperwork was signed on March 3, 2005 with the mighty delta changing hands for "a nominal fee".

Marshall Aerospace and VTST concluded an agreement early in May 2005 that moved the process from 'passive' to 'active'. Within the 'Butler' hangar, the workspace was turned into one that met the stringent requirements of the CAA. This included the institution of bonded stores, clear 'paper trails' and safety parameters. Teams from Marshall and VOC would be working in the same environment as found in any aircraft factory.

From August 2005, the Vulcan was given a full RAF-style overhaul, which the VOC called a 'Major plus', estimated to take at least a year. An Operational Requirement was drafted to examine what was needed on a 21st century Vulcan, and what wasn't. For example, a large amount of the electrical looming related to defensive and offensive systems, which were clearly redundant. A complex set of wiring was discovered, labelled 'mine-laying' – nobody even knew that the bomber was ever intended for such a role.

It was not just a case of stripping out all that was unwanted; there was a weight and balance problem to be considered. The cavernous nose once carried the radar - for the Vulcan's new career 400lb (181kg) of ballast would sit in its place.

Courtesy of the Avro Heritage Centre at the Vulcan's birthplace, Woodford near Manchester, the nose section of B.2 XM602 arrived on October 13, 2005. This would enable constant reference to a fully equipped cockpit, as the instruments and controls were re-installed into XH558. It also permitted the flight crew to go through procedure checks to help get them up to speed for the day they would strap into a 'live' Vulcan again.

ON THE BRINK

Although the engineers had found nothing insurmountable, the pioneering work was taking longer than had been hoped. This was, after all, the largest and most complex return to flight strategy ever attempted – anywhere. All of this was stretching economic resources. The longer it took to put the bomber in the air, the more likely major corporate benefactors would hold back. A vicious spiral was developing.

A jet-like whine was heard in the hangar in May 2006. It was not an Olympus spooling-up, but it was the first time a refitted auxiliary power unit had come to life on XH558 since the 1990s. Rectification work had reached the halfway mark and the recovery phase – putting gear back in – had started.

While the hangar was buzzing and the Vulcan was beginning once again to look like a V-bomber and not a carcass, the fiscal clock was ticking ever faster. May saw the anticipated shortfall hit £850,000. At the end of July a regular review of liabilities showed that things would grind to a halt within four weeks. The trustees had no choice but to make sure that VTST did not become insolvent; the only option was to shut down the project. It was crunch time...

On August 1 the 30 full-time employees were given a month's notice. By this point the figure needed to keep going was £1.2 million. The despondency was tangible.

Robert announced that on August 30, XH558 would roll out no matter what – perhaps to a new beginning, but if nothing transpired then it would be ready for the scrapman. The publicity machine went into overdrive

and soon the Vulcan's plight was international news.

Volunteers from the supporters' club got together to mastermind a response to the crisis. Incalculable hours were spent phoning, mailing, cajoling. As with the days after the lottery bid, pledges were needed that hopefully would be honoured.

A quick calculation based upon a 'magic' number established that if 1,250 people donated £558 each, then, as club chairman Geoffrey Pool said, "we would be home and dry". Those special figures were reflected in the humbling response, be it £5.58, £55.80 or £558. From a standing start, by the time August 30 arrived £870,000 worth of pledges were in hand and £200,000 in cash.

In the week leading up to the poignant roll-out, patriot and philanthropist Sir Jack Hayward – saviour of the SS Great Britain project – had weighed in with a donation of £500,000. He was not known as 'Union Jack' for nothing! All of this meant that the make-or-break event became a joyous occasion.

AS LONG AS IT TAKES

As 2007 dawned, the aircraft was starting to look not just whole, but 'live'. In February the flight crew began to use the cockpit of B.2 XM602 for procedure training. This was in readiness for taxying in the Wellesbourne Mountford example, XM655.

Winter gave way to spring and the mood in the hangar could best be summarised as frustrations countered by patience. It was discovered that there was a need to carry out rectification of the stringers in the main undercarriage bays. This was a relatively simple task, but time-consuming.

Engineering manager Andrew Edmondson brought his philosophy to the fore over the delays: "When it comes down to it, there is something you cannot escape from – the job takes as long as it takes." Robert Pleming was of the same mind: "The enthusiasm, drive and commitment are huge but nobody will jeopardise this unique project – safety and integrity remain paramount."

In May the first engines were fitted, with the others going in early the following month. Work on the cockpit, always seen as the last major phase, was also in hand – the new installation for the GPS system and modern radio rig were tried out.

On June 26, 2007 the Vulcan was taken outside for fuel tests. The complex tanks and pumps were evaluated and the airframe was defuelled to 40% for a thorough inspection. Meanwhile undercarriage retraction was being proven, and the engines and associated systems tried, inspected and tried again.

Complete in every respect, XH558 was rolled out again on August 16, this time for ground running. Dry and wet starts of each Olympus were performed and four days later full power runs were the order of the day – the bird was alive!

Working long hours, the maintenance and support teams clicked their way through all the work cards that needed to be cleared before flight testing could start.

In the first week of September the irrepressible crew chief Cpl Kevin 'Taff' Stone – he was XH558's 'Chiefy' for its final RAF years – noted that there were still 1,000 cards to go through.

All this served to prove the restoration 'law': when the weight of the paperwork equals that of the airframe, all is ready to go.

More ground runs on September 6 went as smooth as silk. Then on the 13th - it would be, wouldn't it? – hydraulic lines failed above No.3 Olympus. That weekend the team got that engine out in just seven hours – not bad as they were only used putting them in. The fault was rectified and the turbojet was re-installed. Undercarriage retraction trials were necessary again – safety, safety, and then safety – and it was back outside for more runs.

All looked fine, but a sub-assembly had to be returned to an OEM for some work. This was achieved in double-quick time. Inspection, refit and a further inspection followed. Suddenly, it dawned on everyone that this ground-breaking and mammoth project was ready.

The flight crew was summoned and prepared XH558 for taxi runs. First at a slow pace, up to 90kts, and then fast - 120kts - with the nosewheel up in the air, decelerating by streaming the braking 'chute. These trials were completed on October 17. The skies of Leicestershire beckoned... And so, all was ready for the event described at the beginning of this feature - Britain's aviation heritage would never be the same again. ○

"THE SKIES OF LEICESTERSHIRE BECKONED... AND SO, ALL WAS READY FOR THE EVENT DESCRIBED AT THE BEGINNING OF THIS FEATURE - BRITAIN'S AVIATION HERITAGE WOULD NEVER BE THE SAME AGAIN."

The Vulcan 'Effect'

Hugh Trevor describes XH558's crowd-pulling flying seasons

Ten years of determination and vision were validated on October 18, 2007 when Vulcan B.2 XH558 thundered down the runway at Bruntingthorpe, Leicestershire, for its inaugural post-restoration test flight. Further sorties led to a Permit to Fly being granted on July 3, 2008.

Time was tight as the Waddington International Airshow weekend was only two days later. Accordingly XH558 arrived in the Lincolnshire airfield's overhead later that same day and carried out a sequence of routines which gained its aircrew a Display Authorisation (DA) to be gained. The 'Cold War' bomber had returned to its spiritual home, having spent much of its operational life with the Waddington Wing.

Its airshow debut on July 5 saw Waddington's Saturday attendance figures eclipse all previous records, 70,000-plus people visiting on that day alone. The 'Vulcan Effect' had begun! The big delta's distinctive planform was displayed to the excited crowd and later two Avro bombers were seen together in the sky as XH558 took part in a flypast led by Lancaster PA474 of the Battle of Britain Memorial Flight (BBMF). Alas, a technical fault on the Sunday prevented the Vulcan taking to the air and the disappointed crowd had to be content with a fast-taxi run.

JUBILATION TO FRUSTRATION

Initial jubilation at getting XH558 into the air following its challenging restoration turned to doubt and disappointment during the 'season' due to technical problems and the weather.

August was a month of frustration, as Vulcan to the Sky Trust (VTST) CEO Dr Robert Pleming described: "We suffered three unrelated technical problems – a brake pipe failure, fuse failures during start-up and the failure of a gear

door retraction jack attachment bracket – which caused XH558 to miss five airshows over three weekends… This was obviously hugely disappointing to expectant audiences and airshow organisers, for which we can only apologise."

In addition to engineering costs, VTST lost more than £50,000 in appearance fees and merchandise profits, which hit hard financially.

September was better, but the Duxford, Cambs, and Leuchars, Scotland, shows were hit by the weather. As a civilian, XH558 was limited to Visual Meteorological Conditions (VMC), effectively a minimum cloudbase of 2,000ft

"THE V-BOMBER'S AIRSHOW DEBUT ON JULY 5 SAW WADDINGTON'S SATURDAY ATTENDANCE FIGURES ECLIPSE ALL PREVIOUS RECORDS, 70,000-PLUS PEOPLE VISITING ON THAT DAY ALONE. THE 'VULCAN EFFECT' HAD BEGUN!"

Above
From March 2011 the Vulcan was based at Robin Hood Airport, previously RAF Finningley. Fifty years before that, XH558 arrived at Finningley, serving with 230 Operational Conversion Unit. DARREN HARBAR

(600m) and minimum visibility of 3 miles (5km).

On November 12, XH558 was ferried from Farnborough, Hampshire, where a brake problem had prolonged its stay after the biennial airshow, to its base at Bruntingthorpe. Ultimately the Vulcan achieved just six public flying displays and a private RAF event in its debut year.

The continued absence of a major sponsor led Robert Pleming to utter some chilling words: "We need to raise about £1.6 million per year, but... the economic conditions are currently the worst they could be. XH558's flying career could still be saved if a few high-profile people came forward with offers of help. However, to be realistic, it looks as if the door may now be closing on the future of the Vulcan in flight."

A 'Save the Vulcan' campaign was launched, but XH558 would not fly again unless funding of £1 million was raised by early 2009.

'PEOPLE POWER'

For the second time in the history of the project, on February 9, 2009 VTST issued redundancy notices to its staff – the clock was ticking. On March 6 the Vulcan was towed out into the spring sunshine at Bruntingthorpe for a press call.

The team knew that the previous week the total raised stood at £480,000 – well short of the target.

When the reality hit home that only public donations would put the mighty delta into the sky for a second season, they rolled in at £8,000 per hour. After much nail-biting, the incredible sum of £956,835 was achieved by the March 6 deadline and, beaming to the cameras, Robert declared that XH558 would fly – "because the public want it to; it truly is the 'People's Aircraft. Never has one aircraft owed so much to so many!" Crew training started that very afternoon.

Since its inception, Vulcan XH558's display routine has developed considerably. Martin Withers describes the evolution: "We always start off flying the previous display routine just to get our hands back in, so to speak. Since we started flying the displays they've got longer and better every year. We do a lot more now than we did in 2008, and you certainly get more noise for your money!

"Flying her is certainly never a burden - I just enjoy it too much. I will miss it enormously when it's over. Having been part of this team for so long it will feel like a huge void. I take no credit whatsoever in getting the Vulcan flying again - but we will look back on it, without a doubt, as a tremendous thing to have done."

Above
The Vulcan dominated the flying at the Goodwood Festival, July 2013.
PHIL WHALLEY-AVPICS

Right
At Robin Hood Airport, XH558 moved into the same hangars it had occupied in the 1960s.
DARREN HARBAR

Sqn Ldr Martin Withers DFC had joined the flight crew; he had been in command of 'Black Buck 1', the raid that bombed the runway at Port Stanley during the Falklands conflict in 1982. Describing his return to the cockpit of a Vulcan after so many years, he said: "It was like riding a bike to a degree – exactly as I remembered. I've had stints as a co-pilot, captain and instructor on Vulcans and it was my one and only operational aircraft. It's actually a nice and straightforward jet to fly. In fact it's a joy to be at the controls ... it really does handle extremely well."

BRUNTINGTHORPE DEPARTURE

The Vulcan deployed to RAF Brize Norton, Oxfordshire, on June 12, 2009 to complete its Civil Aviation Authority aircrew DA process. With this sortie, the delta bade farewell to Bruntingthorpe, its home since March 1993. Two days after arriving at 'Brize' it carried out a formation flypast with a pair of Vickers VC-10s at the station's Families Day. It

"...ALL 380,000 PEOPLE ROSE TO THEIR FEET EN MASSE IN ANTICIPATION. AS THE GIANT V-BOMBER FLEW PAST THERE WERE CHEERS AND CLAPPING. THE 'EFFECT' HAD STRUCK AGAIN!"

then appeared at the RAF Cosford Airshow in Shropshire before venturing overseas for the first time as a civilian to display at Volkel in the Netherlands.

Bad news was to follow; XH558 missed the prestigious Waddington Airshow on July 3/4. Its Permit to Fly had not been renewed in time as structural inspections were incomplete. Robert Pleming apologised and also promised to improve VTST's communications.

Permit issued, a week later XH558 flew to Yeovilton, Somerset, but its display was again cancelled due to unserviceability. But it performed successfully on both days of the Royal International Air Tattoo at Fairford, Glos, the following weekend.

Later that month the tranquil waters and rolling hills of the Lake District were bathed in glorious sunshine as XH558 appeared high to the north above Ambleside, descended towards Windermere and then made its first low pass near Bowness before going into a full display.

Pilots Martin Withers and Kev Rumens had a unique and enviable perspective. Martin recalled: "Our flight over Windermere was superb from the inside. I'd flown there before and the display centre point is the little island right opposite Ambleside, but there's a great big hill about 800ft high in the way, so we knew we'd have to do a different display to that we normally do. We couldn't go up it, as that would mean we'd be constantly ascending and descending, but we discovered we could go *around* it."

WALL OF FIRE

The Victory Show at Cosby, south of Leicester, on September 5 was also spectacular. A re-enactment of the Black Buck bombing runs on the Argentine-occupied Port Stanley airfield was played out, with a massive 'wall of flame' marking the end of the display. Appropriately the sortie was also flown by Falklands veteran Martin Withers.

He recalled the pyrotechnics: "I said I'd run through at about 250 knots and as soon as we'd gone through they'd be clear to set them off. They ended up taking that rather literally! We had throttled back at the time and the noise certainly shook the aeroplane – we felt it and heard it, which I hadn't quite expected. Of course, on the real Black Buck mission we were a lot higher, so it wasn't particularly representative."

A late August weekend saw Bournemouth's seafront unusually crowded as people massed for the Dorset town's airshow, sitting on deckchairs and on the warm sand. In the distance and silhouetted in the sky grew an unmistakable shape. The Vulcan began its run in and, for the first and only time that day, all 380,000 people rose to their feet en masse in anticipation. As the giant V-bomber flew past there were cheers and clapping. The 'Effect' had struck again!

Martin then took XH558 on a 90-mile transit along the south coast to the Devon resort of Dawlish for a memorable flypast, with the nine crimson HS Hawks of the 'Red Arrows' clinging to the vast wings.

"I hadn't even seen Dawlish before, so to run in and see it for the first time with the Red Arrows hanging on to me was both challenging and thrilling," he said. "It's just a little show based around a bay rather than an airfield, so it's not the easiest thing to do and I think it bounced them around a bit. However, it was a wonderful thing to have done and for people to have seen."

50TH BIRTHDAY

Despite XH558's steep funding requirements, in late October 2009 there was a strong sense of optimism in VTST. Barely six months before, the project had faced being wound up, but they had just experienced the kind of airshow season they could barely have dreamt of.

Robert Pleming noted: "XH558 flew a shade under 50 hours, went to 33 events and was seen by just over 2.5 million people… We achieved what we set out to do."

The Trust still needed to raise £400,000 by the close of the year and a further £400,000 by Easter 2010. "It's obviously a big concern that, at some point, goodwill might run out and supporters might tire of dipping into their pockets. The aim was to reach an audience beyond the loyal core of aviation enthusiasts."

Annual baseline costs were around £1.8 million, including rental charges at RAF Lyneham, Wiltshire, where the bomber was based, but additional tasks had increased this

for XH588 and VTST was on the lookout. Bruntingthorpe's role as a vehicle proving ground, with heavy use of the tarmac, risked foreign object damage. Lyneham was satisfactory on a temporary basis but the aim was to have the Vulcan project in its own hangar at a commercial airfield, enabling the Trust to have its own shop and to create a commercial package around it.

By January 2010 winter maintenance was under way at Lyneham. To celebrate XH558's 50th birthday in May 2010 a VTST appeal had reached £175,000 – some £25,000 below the Christmas target, and a total of £800,000 was needed

> "THE CHOICE OF ROBIN HOOD AIRPORT WAS WHOLLY APPROPRIATE AS ITS PREVIOUS INCARNATION WAS RAF FINNINGLEY… AIR TRAFFIC CONTROL GREETED THE NEW RESIDENT WITH 'WELCOME HOME' AS THE VULCAN TOUCHED DOWN."

by £800,000. Martin Withers remarked: "People perhaps forget we've been flying this aircraft for two years now. Things are getting worn out and it's quite normal that those things now need to be replaced, or at least looked at."

The airframe had reached 250 of its 320 'fatigue units' of life, meaning the next life extension modifications were imminent. Robert Pleming explained: "That'll require two modifications: the strengthening of the main spar bottom booms, and the landing lamp apertures on each wing. Then there's the engine life management… because, assuming all the structural fatigue issues are addressed, the first thing that could stop us flying is the powerplant."

A new home was also needed

by March 31. Moving the VTST offices to Hinckley, Leicestershire, and hangaring the aircraft at Lyneham was saving £10,000 a month, but significant corporate sponsorship remained elusive. Fortunately, in March an anonymous £400,000 donation was received, effectively saving the project.

SPIRIT OF GREAT BRITAIN

After completion of the winter maintenance programme, including the major modification to the spar, the bomber flew from Lyneham to Brize Norton on July 1, 2010 prior to successful displays at Waddington and at Goodwood, Sussex. Following XH558's half-century in May the Vulcan proudly bore the moniker *The Spirit of Great Britain.*

It was estimated that more than a million people saw XH558 fly in 2010, but a substantial drop in donations during the recession, together with poor weather that stopped attendance at several profitable events, led VTST to develop a business plan to provide greater commercial revenue – as £365,000 was required by the end of October.

Robert Pleming said at the time: "It will allow us to increase the role the Vulcan plays in teaching science, technology, maths and 'Cold War' history, and in inspiring the young engineers of the future. Today, though, 2011 looks a long way away."

Yet again, in the nick of time donations rolled into Hinckley at the rate of £30,000 each day. "The response to our winter appeal has been quite remarkable," said Robert. "In little more than a month, we went from being threatened with closure to having sufficient funds to maintain [XH558] through the winter."

WELCOME HOME

Searches for a new operating base bore fruit on March 29, 2011 when XH558 arrived at Doncaster Sheffield Robin Hood Airport in Yorkshire. Martin Withers brought the aircraft in for a low, wheels-down flypast before making a circuit and landing assisted by

the brake 'chute. The spectacle was witnessed with delight by enthusiasts and veterans – and with bemusement by passengers waiting for their flights to sunnier climes.

The choice of Robin Hood Airport was wholly appropriate as its previous incarnation was RAF Finningley, where XH558 was delivered on July 1, 1960 to begin its – and the B.2 variant's – career with 230 Operational Conversion Unit. Air traffic control greeted the new resident with 'Welcome home' as the Vulcan touched down.

Martin later described it as "one of the most emotional experiences of my life".

The delta would be housed and maintained in the same hangar that serviced it half a century before.

Alas, technical issues in August meant the Vulcan missed around a month's worth of revenue-earning appearances and associated merchandising. A fuel tank problem led to its removal and despatch for repair; then a hydraulic failure

Left
Crowds were always impressed with XH558's fighter-like manoeuvrability – Little Gransden, August 2014.
PHIL WHALLEY-AVPICS

occurred during a DA flight at Cottesmore, Rutland.

Engineering director Andrew Edmondson explained: "We had enough power to get the gear down for landing, but... it was a Sunday and the only airfield available to us with crash facilities was Coningsby [where] we changed the seal and a hydraulic pump, did all the functionality tests and eventually flew out."

Fortunately the rest of the 2011 season went well, but another funding shortfall led to major equipment overhauls being delayed during the winter service, which was forecast to cost £400,000. Components in six major systems had reached the end of their service life and needed to be stripped, inspected and overhauled. Additionally, the braking parachutes were 20 years old and needed replacing.

Fortunately, more than £100,000 raised during February 2012, gave VTST the confidence to send vital items such as ejection seats to specialist suppliers for refurbishment.

HITTING THE TARGET

Demands on XH558 during 2012 included the 30th anniversary of the Falklands conflict, Andrew Edmondson commenting: "We're

determined to be in the air to commemorate the remarkable Black Buck mission by Vulcan and Victor crews."

Events 60 years before were also to be celebrated: the Diamond Jubilee of Her Majesty the Queen and the inaugural test flight of the prototype Vulcan by 'Roly' Falk.

Once again, XH558 hit the target and was back in the air in April, performing flypasts over 400 former V-bomber personnel at the Newark Air Museum in Nottinghamshire, which was hosting a 'Tribute to the V-Force' event.

For pilot Martin Withers there was an especially poignant occasion on May 20 with the opportunity to pay tribute to the men who lost their lives in the South Atlantic. Despite the overcast weather, the recently repainted Vulcan gleamed as it flew over the National Memorial Arboretum at Alrewas, Staffordshire, for the dedication of the Falklands Memorial.

As a veteran of the conflict, this was a special moment for Martin: "My wife was there and a lot of people reported how moving it was to have the Vulcan fly over," he said.

"I prefer to call it the liberation of the Falklands because that's how the islanders refer to it. It does feel

strange that 30 years after I flew a Vulcan operationally I'm still flying one of the old girls today and I feel incredibly honoured and privileged to be doing so."

DEVASTATED

Calamity struck just eight days later. Less than a week before XH558 was due to achieve the major goal of participation in the River Thames Pageant of the Queen's Diamond Jubilee celebrations, there was a double engine failure at the start of the take-off roll for a training flight. The crew immediately abandoned the run, shut down the two affected powerplants and taxied clear of the runway.

Bags of silica gel desiccant, used to help dry out the engines between flights, had been ingested by the No.1 (port outer) Olympus which surged and suffered compressor blade failure, debris from which caused the No.2 to fail.

Robert Pleming was candid about the incident which wrecked two valuable engines beyond repair: "We're a close team and everyone here is devastated. We're in a state of shock."

Despite this major setback the crew set about installing two new Olympus 202s. Just five weeks later XH558 returned to the sky to resume the appearance schedule. Robert explained: "The error was down to a combination of factors but we've put measures in place to stop anything similar happening again. We were terribly disappointed to have missed the River Thames Diamond Jubilee Pageant on June 3, but as it turned out the weather was so appalling that day that we'd never have been able to get down there anyway."

Following a display at Clacton in Essex on August 23, XH558 overflew Southend Airport to celebrate the 50th anniversary of the Vulcan Restoration Trust's resident B.2 XL426 – and on September 9 it made two low passes over B.2 XM603 at the Avro Heritage Centre at Woodford, south of Manchester, to commemorate the first flight of the Vulcan prototype, VX770. In September it also had the honour of opening the Farnborough International Airshow in the company of the Red Arrows.

AGAINST THE ODDS

As the new year dawned, the VTST team knew it would end with many challenges to face. "By the end of 2013 we will have reached a stage where major modifications are needed," said Robert Pleming. "It would be a demanding and expensive operation to strengthen a section of the leading edge of both wings... I want to emphasise that if we *can* fly on into 2014, we absolutely intend to do so."

With support from Cranfield Aerospace, the VTST engineering team designed reinforcement plates for the leading edges – 2013 was *not* going to be XH558's swansong, and the first sortie of the year was flown in May.

Unfortunately a leak in the No.2 fuel tank in the forward fuselage grounded the Vulcan towards the end of the season. A new tank would

have to be manufactured, which would take 16 weeks.

Funds required for the tank, the wing mods and winter servicing totalled £800,000 but, as had so often happened in the past, a public appeal enabled the financial target to be reached. The Beagle Technology Group set about producing the wing plates and by the end of May 2014 the Vulcan was airborne again. Even with all this achieved, it was clear that lack of engine life would almost certainly preclude flying beyond the end of 2015.

Robert noted: "The main constraint is on the engines: we're very carefully managing and monitoring that and Rolls-Royce has been incredibly helpful. This year [2014] we're trying to change the way we operate the aircraft, effectively trading off fatigue life against engine life. We've changed the way we fly XH558 and if anything it should look a little more attractive as we're flying quite a bit faster."

At that point VTST still had six airworthy Olympus 202s – four installed and two awaiting their turn. By careful husbanding, enough hours on the two spares allowed for a single ferry flight. If, for example, a bird strike were to take out both engines on one side, there would still be two engines to take the delta back to base, so it would not be instantly grounded.

THREE AVROS

The highlight of 2014 was the Vulcan's series of flypasts on August 21 with Lancasters PA474 of BBMF and KB726 of the Canadian Warplane Heritage on the latter's unique transatlantic visit. The three Avro bombers took off from Waddington and flew together over nearby Canwick Hill before heading to Metheringham and Coningsby in Lincolnshire and on to Marham in Norfolk.

The flights were timed to coincide with a turf-cutting ceremony for the memorial at the International Bomber Command Centre at Canwick Hill. This was within sight of Lincoln Cathedral, once a landmark for crews returning from raids over Europe.

Bill Ramsey, XH558's captain for the historic flight, said: "I don't think there's much doubt that this will be my favourite-ever day in aviation." His feelings were echoed by the Canadian Lancaster pilot, Dave Rohrer: "This is quite an honour. For us to have the last two Lancasters in the world and the only Vulcan in the world, all Avro, is amazing. To fly three ships like this in 2014, I don't think anyone could have dreamed it."

Two generations of Avro bombers in the sky together was certainly dream-like. But the Vulcan had already flown for far longer than anyone ever expected; the bubble was bound to burst before long... ◉

"THIS IS QUITE AN HONOUR. FOR US TO HAVE THE LAST TWO LANCASTERS IN THE WORLD AND THE ONLY VULCAN IN THE WORLD, ALL AVRO, IS AMAZING. TO FLY THREE SHIPS LIKE THIS IN 2014, I DON'T THINK ANYONE COULD HAVE DREAMED IT."

Final Countdown

Everyone knew the delta dream had to come to an end — Hugh Trevor reviews the emotional last season and the farewell tour

"Having evaluated a great many factors, the three expert companies on whom we depend [BAE Systems, Marshall Aerospace and Defence Group, and Rolls-Royce] —known as the 'technical authorities' — have together decided to cease their support at the end of this flying 'season'. Without that support, under Civil Aviation Authority [CAA] regulations, we are prohibited from flying." So began the Vulcan to the Sky Trust (VTST) press release of May 15, 2015.

It continued: "At the heart of their decision are two factors. First, although we are all confident that XH558 is currently as safe as any aircraft flying today, her structure and systems are already more than

10% beyond the flying hours of any other Vulcan, so knowing where to look for any possible failure is becoming more difficult. These can be thought of as the 'unknown unknown' issues, which can be impossible to predict with any accuracy. Second, maintaining her superb safety record requires expertise that is increasingly difficult to find.

"Our technical partners already bring specialists out of retirement specifically to work on XH558, a solution that is increasingly impractical for those businesses as the necessary skills become distant in their collective memories. We have recently been made aware that the skills issue is particularly acute as our engines age and will require a considerable amount of additional (and costly) inspection and assessment."

Everyone knew the time would come, but the news was still greeted with sorrow. The VTST team set to creating the 'Farewell to Flight' scheme, designed to give XH558 the best *ever* display season and to put in train planning for a national finale in October. (See the panel overleaf for XH558's crowded commitments in 2015.)

V-FORCE SALUTE

A nationwide 'Salute to the V-Force' tour was carried out on June 27/28, flying XH558 over every intact Vulcan, Victor and Valiant in the UK - 17 sites in all, see page 34. On the 27th, Martin Withers, Kev Rumens and Jonathan Lazzari took the Vulcan on a three-hour circuit of the northerly sites, including Woodford, near Manchester where XH558 had its maiden flight in May 1960.

Indifferent weather forecasts did not stop Bill Perrins, Phil O'Dell and Phil Davies from touring the southerly locations the following day; concluding with an appearance at the Cleethorpes airshow. Huge numbers of enthusiastic Vulcan well-wishers congregated around the former V-force sites to greet XH558. This was a sign of what was to come: 'People Power' had helped the delta take flight, it would mass to bid it farewell.

VTST CEO Robert Pleming commented: "To say that the tour was a success is somewhat of an understatement... [with] a packed season ahead it's certainly turning into a summer to remember".

So it proved to be. Highlights including formation flypasts with the de Havilland Sea Vixen and two Norwegian Vampires at Yeovilton Air Day and several with the 'Red Arrows'.

> "UPON LOWERING THE UNDERCARRIAGE, THE CUSTOMARY GREEN LIGHTS TO CONFIRM THE MAIN GEAR HAD LOCKED DOWN LIT UP ON THE INSTRUMENT PANEL; BUT THE NOSEWHEEL LIGHT REMAINED RED SIGNIFYING THE LEG HAD FAILED TO EXTEND FULLY."

Above right
Saluting Durham Tees Valley Airport, the former RAF Middleton St George, on October 10.
GEOFF HILL

SHADOW OF SHOREHAM

Sadly, a long shadow was cast over the latter part of the 'season' by the tragic crash of Hawker Hunter T.7 G-BXFI at Shoreham, Sussex, on August 22, which resulted in the deaths of 11 people and injuries to 16 more. This led the CAA to introduce temporary restrictions limiting vintage jet aircraft to 'flat' flypasts over land.

After careful consideration, the VTST team was able to incorporate subtle changes to the Vulcan display to comply with the new ruling. While this somewhat limited the wingovers, it preserved the much-loved engine howl, as experienced at Rhyl and Dunsfold on the following weekend.

Pilot Bill Ramsey reported on the new flight regime on the August 29/30 weekend: "With Kev Rumens as captain, we flew one of our longest trips so far. The displays at Dunsfold and Dartmouth were flown by Kev and me respectively under the terms of the CAA Safety Note following the [Shoreham] accident. This restricted angle of bank for us, but hopefully didn't spoil peoples' enjoyment of the displays. I was still able to fly our normal display at Rhyl in brilliant sunshine, which was highly enjoyable as it was probably my last 'unrestricted' display.

"On Sunday 30 ...this time with me as captain, we tried to beat the forecast weather to fulfil our display commitments. Unfortunately, the front lying across the country meant the cloud base and visibility in heavy rain fell below our VMC [visual meteorological conditions] limits ten miles or so south of Melton Mowbray — causing us to turn around.

"We tried to go east to find a route through East Anglia, but to no avail. Given the complex and busy airspace in the vicinity of Heathrow, Farnborough and Gatwick the use of the IMC [instrument meteorological conditions] clearance was impractical, especially at very short notice. I'm sorry for those who were disappointed but we had no choice."

Prior to a display at Clacton on August 27, VTST seized the opportunity to create another unique formation when, at the invitation of base commander Colonel Robert Novotny, the V-bomber performed three passes over Lakenheath, Suffolk, accompanied by a pair of F-15C Eagles of the USAF 48th Fighter Wing on the wingtips.

TWO GREENS

Following successful displays at Portrush, Northern Ireland, and Ayr, Scotland, on September 5, Bill Perrins, Phil O'Dell and Phil Davies were in the circuit to land at Prestwick. Upon lowering the undercarriage, the customary green lights to confirm the main gear had locked down lit up on the instrument panel; but the nosewheel light remained red signifying the leg had failed to extend fully. This situation was confirmed by a Battle of Britain Memorial Flight Spitfire pilot flying alongside.

Fortunately, 'three greens' were eventually achieved and, after visual confirmation from the Spitfire of full leg extension, a successful landing was made — the nose being held off for as long as possible. Unfortunately, this led to cancellation of the Ayr and Cosby displays on the following day as XH558 transited back to base— with landing gear locked down. At Robin Hood Airport, XH558's Yorkshire base, further investigation of the undercarriage deployment and retraction system was carried out. The suspicion was that air had entered the hydraulic system via a faulty fitting.

Unserviceability caused more dismay the following weekend with missed appearances at Goodwood and Old Sarum. While holding over the South Downs a suspected fuel leak dictated a decision to return to base. A gauging error was always considered a possibility, and so it turned out to be, however on-board testing in flight had suggested otherwise. With safety always a priority the captain elected to return to Robin Hood.

With the glitch cured, the delta was test flown on September 13, enabling XH558 to keep its date with the Vulcan to the Sky Club at Coventry for a special occasion. This was a 'thank you' to the thousands of dedicated members, many of whom had supported the project since the beginning. A variety of events were laid on, including signing sessions by former 'Black Buck' aircrew and displays by aircraft of the based Classic Air Force.

CLOCK TICKING

With the clock ticking, the fine weather which blessed Southport on Merseyside on September 19 allowed Kev Rumens, Martin Withers and Jonathan Lazzari to demonstrate the Vulcan's startling manoeuvrability with a last, unrestricted, howling display over the sea — including a spiral climb, absent from the recent routine — and concluding with Kev's trademark wingover.

Providing the scarlet icing on the cake, spectators at Southport were also privileged to witness the final Vulcan formation flypast with the 'Red Arrows'. Was it imagination or was the formation a little tighter than at Fairford?

Leeds East Airport, formerly RAF Church Fenton, opened its gates to welcome the Vulcan on Saturday September 26, holding its first major air display since 1994. The gleaming delta flew a poignant formation with

the Gnat Display Team, a colourful dart clinging to each wingtip in tribute to Kevin Whyman, the third member of the team, who tragically lost his life in August during a display. As XH558 disappeared heavenwards and the earth stopped shaking, spontaneous applause broke out — accompanied by grown men surreptitiously wiping away tears…

Back at Robin Hood, large crowds - estimated at more than 3,000 - congregated, heavily disrupting the day-to-day function of the airport. Robert Pleming announced: "I must ask everyone, please do not come to Robin Hood to see her take-off and land. If numbers are vast, the police may have no option but to lock down the airport, the financial consequences of which to the trust would be terminal."

Accordingly, VTST did not publicise XH558's attendance at the unveiling ceremony for the Spire Memorial at the International Bomber Command Centre, Lincoln, until an hour before flight. The private ceremony took place in front of more than 300 World War Two veterans on October 2, with the Vulcan making a unique contribution.

The very last 'formal' display of a crowded season was overhead at Shuttleworth Collection's wonderful all-grass aerodrome at Old Warden, Bedfordshire. The Vulcan had performed here on July 5 and as then, there was a capacity crowd

to greet the delta. Sharp-eyed spectators saw that Martin Withers was on the ground and in conclave with Shuttleworth's chief pilot 'Dodge' Bailey. The Vulcan closed the show and Martin took to the microphone to introduce it and an exceptional 'formation'.

Built in 1946, Avro XIX G-AHKX flew for a brief while with XH558 off its starboard wing. The XIX, a post-war civil version of the famed Anson, could trace its roots back to 1935. Avro's incredible gifted designer, Roy Chadwick, schemed the Anson and had his hand in the format adopted by the Vulcan - a connection well appreciated by the audience.

NATIONAL FINALE

From late September the VTST website announced that over the weekend of October 10/11 XH558 would carry out the most extensive national tour to allow as many people as possible to see the delta for the last time.

Chief Pilot Martin Withers spent much time optimising the north and south 'farewell' tours: "Both flights are amongst the longest she has undertaken since the restoration." This was very ambitious, even with GPS and other navigation aids, it represented a spectacular piece of flying - both sorties coming to just over seven hours of flying time.

The northern sector, stages on the 10th took in around 28 waypoints,

VULCAN FLIGHT CREW 2015

Martin Withers DFC - VTST Chief Pilot Air Operations Manager: Joined the RAF in 1968 and flew Vulcan B.2s on 44 and 50 Squadrons. Became a Qualified Flying Instructor (QFI) on Jet Provosts and on the Vulcans with 230 OCU, later becoming 101 Squadron QFI and Pilot Leader at Waddington. In 1982 took part in Operation 'Corporate', the Falklands Conflict, being awarded the DFC for 'Black Buck 1', the bombing of Port Stanley runway in Vulcan B.2 XM607.

Martin Withers (left) and Andy Marson. DARREN HARBAR

Martin concluded his RAF career instructing at Linton-on-Ouse before becoming an airline pilot.

Kevin Rumens - Pilot: Joined the RAF in 1984 and flew Victor K.2s on 55 Squadron. He displayed XH558 for two seasons with the RAF Vulcan Display Flight, before instructing on Jet Provosts and Tucanos. He completed a Fast Jet Crossover and flew Tornado GR.1s on 14 Squadron, later instructing on the GR.1 at Lossiemouth and converting to the GR.4. Kev flew combat missions over Iraq, policing the no-fly zones after the first Gulf War and missions in the second Gulf War. He retired from the RAF in 2004 and flies Airbus A340s for Virgin.

Bill Ramsey - Pilot: Joined the RAF in 1972, flying Vulcan B.2s on 35 Squadron. He then became a QFI on Jet Provosts before converting to Harriers and Tornado GR.1s. For four years was with the 'Red Arrows'. He retired from the RAF in 2008, becoming a reservist, as a QFI on Tutors with 115 Squadron and was Tutor Display Pilot 2009-2010.

Phil O'Dell - Pilot: Flew Buccaneers as a weapons instructor and QFI on Hawks with operational sorties on Jaguars. He left the RAF in 2001 to join Rolls-Royce and leads the Heritage Flight's Spitfire operation. He flew Airbus A320s and Boeing 777s with British Airways, and also flies a Boeing 747 flying test-bed.

Bill Perrins - Pilot: Joined the RAF in 1974 and flew Vulcan B.2s with 44 Squadron, including Falklands operations. He moved on to Jet Provost and Hawk instructing before converting to Tornado F3s. Bill left the RAF in 1993 and is a training captain with Virgin. He owns a share in a Bücker Jungmann and greatly enjoys displaying Spitfires and Mustangs.

Phil Davies - Lead Air Electronics Officer (AEO): Joined the RAF in 1972, as an AEO on Vulcan B.2s with 44 Squadron before becoming an electronic warfare (EW) specialist. In 1982 Phil was posted to Boscombe Down on trials supporting the Falklands Campaign and the Vulcan tanker. For the latter he flew heavyweight take-off and landing trials in XH558. Following a NATO EW appointment he joined 360 Squadron on Canberra T.17s prior to Nimrod R.1 operations in the Middle East and the Balkans. Phil retired from the RAF in 2007.

Jonathan Lazzari - AEO: Joined as an RAF Apprentice and later served on Nimrods before becoming an AEO on Vulcan B.2s with 44 Squadron. After instructional tours he was posted to Canberra T.17s on 360 Squadron. Staff tours involved deployment in support of the Balkans campaign as EW Director on the NATO Battle Staff and finally to Air Command. Jonathan left the RAF in 1999 and currently operates Falcon 20s with Cobham, training all nationalities in the 'art' of air warfare.

> ## "AS XH558 DISAPPEARED HEAVENWARDS AND THE EARTH STOPPED SHAKING, SPONTANEOUS APPLAUSE BROKE OUT — ACCOMPANIED BY GROWN MEN SURREPTITIOUSLY WIPING AWAY TEARS..."

streaming through Yorkshire, the Midlands, XH558's Mancunian birthplace, Lancashire, Cumbria, Scotland and the North East. The next day notched up around 35 venues: Lincolnshire, east London, Kent, Hampshire, Bristol, south Wales, the West Midlands and home to Robin Hood.

The weekend included high-tech solutions to keeping a vast number of people up to date on the 'where' and the all-important 'when'. Post-event, the VTST website described the awesome task: "The huge simultaneous demand for information knocked our website and tracking system servers offline ahead of XH558 becoming airborne. At one point, our records show that we had over 660,000 data requests in the space of a single hour! Luckily, Twitter and Facebook are quite capable of handling such traffic levels and we were able to keep the majority of people informed by social media.

"On Saturday, we had to turn short of running through at East Midlands Airport, so we re-arranged that flypast on the Sunday. When in Bristol airspace, we completed the Severn Bridges out of sequence to the route originally published. XH558 did indeed visit the Severn Bridges after completing a flypast at Llandegfedd Reservoir."

It is estimated that 300,000-plus people witnessed XH558's national 'parade' but reports filtering in since look set to have that figure much

nearer to half-a-million spectators. At North Weald in Essex, the airfield probably witnessed an influx of close on 3,000 visitors with cars taking in excess of an hour to leave afterwards. At Rutland Water's north shore a spokesman put the attendance figure at more than 1,500. Right up to the last minutes, the 'Vulcan Effect' was fully functional!

One of the challenges creating a publication that covers a specific event is the question of when to press the 'go' button. Throughout the production of this special edition of *FlyPast*, close links were maintained with the VTST planners. The national tour 'moved' in the calendar, but settled on the second weekend of October and with that, a date was made with the printers.

The team at Robin Hood had another 'thank you' plotted for XH558's amazing supporters and this was hinted at as October progressed. As *Vulcan Farewell* closed for press it looked as though the delta had acknowledged the national yell of 'Encore!' that followed in its wake as it toured the UK.

By the time these words are read we will all know if, weather and operational circumstances notwithstanding, XH558 took a curtain call to pay its respects to the countless numbers of people who helped to achieve the impossible and the fabulous - the world's most powerful warbird. We will not see anything like it ever again.

Over XH558's first home as a civilian, Bruntingthorpe, with Victor K.2 XM715 'Teasin' Tina' below. JAMIE EWAN

Down but not Out

A new career awaits XH558 at Robin Hood Airport – learn how you can help inspire the future

Right
Hangar 3 is the base for an award-winning team providing visitors with a close view of XH558.

Below
Vulcan XH558 is no stranger to the hangars at Robin Hood Airport. When the airfield was RAF Finningley, it served with the resident 230 Operational Conversion Unit.

After service as a V-bomber in the defence of the nation from 1960 and as an RAF heritage display aircraft between 1984 and 1992, XH558 was retired by the Ministry of Defence. Acquired by David Walton, the delta was ferried to Bruntingthorpe, Leicestershire, in March 1933 to start a new life as a civilian.

In October 2007, the Vulcan to the Sky Trust (VTST) pulled off what many people considered impossible – XH558 took its first test flight, becoming the world's most powerful warbird. By the time these words are read, the Vulcan will have carried out its last-ever flight.

While XH558 is *down*, it is certainly not *out* – great things are expected of it as the centrepiece of a new and exciting project at its base, Robin Hood Airport

in Yorkshire. This new phase of XH558's remarkable life will see a considerable widening of the scope of its operations, providing greater access, more activities and an increased focus on inspiration and education.

This venture has been named the Etna Project. In ancient Roman mythology, Vulcan was the god of fire and metalworking whose forge was said to be within Mount Etna in Sicily. There Vulcan crafted many fine things, including weapons for his fellow deities and the thrones on which they sat on Mount Olympus. (Risking stretching the analogies too far, the V-bomber was propelled by Rolls-Royce *Olympus* turbojets.)

At Robin Hood Airport, the Etna Project will also act as a forge, helping to create new generations of engineers and arming them with the skills needed to excel.

"WHILE XH558 IS *DOWN*, IT IS CERTAINLY NOT *OUT* – GREAT THINGS ARE EXPECTED OF IT AS THE CENTREPIECE OF A NEW AND EXCITING PROJECT..."

FOSTERING AMBITION

People of all ages and interests have visited XH558 in its hangar and made it clear how much they valued being able to get so close to such a powerful and impressive aircraft. While the Vulcan has had to stop flying, the effect it has on the public will not cease. The V-bomber will remain dynamic and alive, providing a powerful reminder of a remarkable era.

Under the leadership of the Aviation Skills Partnership, which runs several aviation skills hubs including the Norwich International Aviation Academy, the Vulcan Aviation Academy will be established. This will provide a 'real world' learning experience to promote the talents needed for youngsters to enter the aerospace industry and to provide them with increased opportunities. The academy will concentrate on six

Left
The Vulcan will be kept in running order and will stage regular under power runs at Robin Hood Airport.

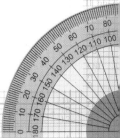

A GLIMPSE OF THE FUTURE

Concept designs for the Etna Centre show the ambition and scope of the long-term element of the project. Here, Vulcan XH558 lovingly maintained in 'live' status, will continue to be the centrepiece.

VTST-BOND BRYAN ARCHITECTS

Right
The mighty delta will be maintained in 'live' condition and regular fast taxi runs will be staged.

areas of expertise: pilot, air traffic, airport operations, flight 'ops', cabin crew and aviation engineering.

The plan is supported by a core group of founding partners including Peel Airports Group, Doncaster College and University Centre, Skypeople, Aviation Shake, the Spirit of Goole Youth Build-a-Plane Project, and the Light Aircraft Association Educational Trust.

Hangar 3, XH558's home, will initially become the Vulcan Heritage Centre. New elements will take visitors close to the aircraft when it is 'power on' and there will be regular fast taxi runs. The history and achievements of V-force, the technology behind the Vulcan and the legacy of the V-bombers will all be included in displays and presentations that can be enjoyed by visitors of all ages.

This will also provide a remarkable environment for private and corporate events. In recent years

VTST developed considerable experience in the hosting of events, with weddings a speciality. The Vulcan is a powerful backdrop for special occasions of all kinds.

An innovation is the Heritage Aircraft Engineering scheme which will build on the skills that the VTST team has developed to administer, maintain and operate complex historic aircraft. The team that looks after the Vulcan has much to offer owners of warbirds, large or small, piston or jet.

Since the inception of VTST, education has been an important facet of the Vulcan's operation. At Bruntingthorpe, and later at Robin Hood, award-winning visitor activities centred on access to the mighty delta, and the people who maintain her have been very popular with schools. In recent years the hangar team has hosted more than 15,000 visitors per year.

BUILDING FOR THE FUTURE

Aviation Skills Partnership is working hard to secure the lease on Hangar 3 at Robin Hood Airport while a new, purpose-built hub is created – this will be the Etna Centre. Co-located on the edge of the airport, with easy access to the taxiways, the Etna Centre is the most ambitious of the VTST's proposals.

This will build on XH558's inspirational qualities to change the perceptions of the young, and those who influence them, through hands-on experience of a wide range of technologies. Phase One of this incredible project is intended to be complete by September 2017. The Etna Centre will be of a size and scope to expand the activities, providing a long-term basis for aviation education and inspiration for many years to come – a fitting tribute to the People's Plane, Vulcan XH558.

"...AWARD-WINNING VISITOR ACTIVITIES CENTRED ON ACCESS TO THE MIGHTY DELTA, AND THE PEOPLE WHO MAINTAIN HER HAVE BEEN VERY POPULAR WITH SCHOOLS. IN RECENT YEARS THE HANGAR TEAM HAS HOSTED MORE THAN 15,000 VISITORS PER YEAR."

Above
Andrew and Kirsty Biddulph had a very special setting for their wedding blessing in October 2014, courtesy of XH558. Hangar 3 offers great possibilities for all kinds of event. *KEITH CAMPBELL*

Above left
The Vulcan Heritage Centre will allow visitors close access to XH558. *ALL DARREN HARBAR UNLESS NOTED*

Don't cry because it's over,
smile
because it happened...

That's how the Vulcan to the Sky Trust website said enthusiasts should react to the news that 2015 was to be XH558's curtain call. Pulling away from the show at Throckmorton, Worcestershire, on June 15, the delta left the audience spellbound and many of them disobeyed the instruction, shedding more than a few tears. ROBERT FALCONER

This special edition of *FlyPast* is dedicated to the organisations and authorities, the companies and businesses, everyone at the Vulcan to the Sky Trust and the Club, the technicians, the specialists, the flight crew, the ground crew, and most importantly of all, every enthusiast – all have helped make the most challenging and complex restoration to fly a reality.